And God said,
"Behold, I have given you every plant
yielding seed that is on the face of all the earth,
and every tree with seed in its fruit.
You shall have them for food."
—Genesis 1:29 ESV

THEEARTHYCANVAS

Vegan COOKBOOK

100+ PLANT-BASED RECIPES THAT TASTE AS GOOD AS THEY LOOK

FAY KAZZI, PhD, MS, RD
author of TheEarthyCanvas

Pacific Press®
Publishing Association
Nampa, Idaho | www.pacificpress.com

Photography & Art Direction: Fay Kazzi
Design & Production: Wendy Hunt

Library of Congress
Cataloging-in-Publication Data

Names: Kazzi, Fay, author.
Title: The Earthy canvas vegan
    cookbook : 100+ plant-based recipes
    that taste as good as they look /
    Fay Kazzi, PhD, MS, RD.
Other titles: Earthy canvas.
Description: [Nampa, Idaho] : Pacific
    Press Publishing Association, 2019. |
    Includes indexes. | Summary:
    "A cookbook containing over one
    hundred plant-based recipes"—
    Provided by publisher.
Identifiers: LCCN 2019040078 |
    ISBN 9780816365982 (paperback)
Subjects: LCSH: Vegan cooking. |
    LCGFT: Cookbooks.
Classification: LCC TX837 .K28 2019 |
    DDC 641.5/6362—dc23
LC record available at https://lccn.loc
    .gov/2019040078

December 2019

This book is dedicated to you.
You who desire to better your
understanding of creating
wholesome meals and making it a
beautiful experience every day.

Contents

INTRODUCTION

HELLO! I'm Fay. I'm part Lebanese and part Egyptian. I spent thirteen years (teenage and early adulthood) living in the Middle East, in the beautiful country of Lebanon, and grew up around an incredibly authentic variety of Eastern cuisines. Whether I was eating Kushari out of a copper plate in an old mom-and-pop shop in the middle of a loud market in Cairo, Egypt, dining the authentic meza spread in an ancient palace courtyard turned restaurant in Damascus, Syria, or eating a freshly baked mankoushe in the Broumana mountains of Lebanon where I lived, one thing is for sure, food in these places with the people I loved produced the most "present" moments I've ever experienced. So, as the inevitable would have it, food would follow me down the path of my education and career.

What God says about food

"Behold, I have given you every plant yielding seed that is on the face of all the earth, and every tree with seed in its fruit. You shall have them for food" (Genesis 1:29, ESV).

When I read this verse, it tells me that God originally intended for our diet to be "plant-based." As time went on and environmental catastrophes limited food options, He permitted humans to partake of animals and animal products, but originally speaking, it was all about plants.

How do I perceive food?

Food, to me, is so much more than taste and smell; it's about reading the intent of the presentation and taking a moment to observe how it makes you feel. Food is also about *you*. It has the power to heal and bring life to your body. I believe healthy food has a divine responsibility to look and taste as good as it can be for you. What we put in our bodies directly affects our minds and, in turn, our spirituality. Also, evidence-based research today on the benefits of plant-based diets is now in the limelight like never before. My mission with this resource is to show how easy, meaningful, and beautiful, healthy food preparation can be!

My story

Ever since I can remember, I've always had a special interest in food. One of my dad's favorite memories of me as a child was on my third birthday, when he asked me if I wanted to have cake, to which I enthusiastically responded: "No, I want a pickle!" And yes, he has it on video! What an odd request for a three-year-old to make on their birthday, you might think! But you see, I loved pickles. Being so high in salt and acid, my mom wouldn't let me have them as often as I would have liked. But on my birthday, I was allowed to have an entire thick, crunchy, cold, dill pickle, just for me. No splitting with my brother or having my mom cut it in half and toss back into the jar all sad and lonely. That doesn't mean I didn't have cake, but that pickle did something in my mouth that cake couldn't do. There was something about the strength of flavors, the unapologetic saltiness that balanced beautifully with a subtle sweetness which married into the acidity of the brine and enveloped its goodness in a firm, cool morsel, coating my entire mouth and tickling the back of my throat with lingering delight. That is my earliest understanding and appreciation of flavor. Today, I can tell you, though, I haven't grown out of my love for pickles, I will still only have them on special occasions; you'd be proud mom, and you're welcome to my kidneys!

As fate would have it, food was going to be the direction my education would take me as I pursued a bachelor of science in nutrition and dietetics, which led me to later complete a master's program in nutrition and dietetics as well. Shortly after receiving my master of science degree (MS), I sat for a grueling exam, which qualified me to become a registered dietitian. Within the same year of graduating with my MS, I was accepted into a PhD program in rehabilitation science, where I geared my research into probiotic therapy for gut rehabilitation. Up until midway through my PhD program, my relationship with food, though enthusiastic and passionate, was limited in its exploration, expression, and identity.

How food became art

I've always been an artist at heart. Diving into the sciences with my education and career was an area in which I needed to invest a lot more intention. Amid the grueling demands of a PhD program, running a clinical trial, and juggling three jobs to pay my way through school, I was praying for some form of a creative outlet, as I was nearing a breaking point. Soon after, my prayer was answered, and I discovered an insatiable love for food photography and recipe creation that somehow seamlessly blended with my existing profession. It was a tremendous stress reliever and the perfect form of recreation I needed. Food styling soon followed, and before I knew it, I was absorbed in the artistic world of aesthetics and presentation, which I am convinced plays an important role in the overall commitment to healthier food and lifestyle-medicine practices. All of the pictures in this book were taken with my Canon Rebel in the humble setting of my little garage studio. The food photography you will see here is very personal, and I went to great lengths to ensure I directed each part and told you the story through my lens and styling techniques as I would want it to be read.

As I continued to study the nutrient content of food, the balancing techniques of flavors, and how to tweak my recipes to capture just the right amount of taste and texture with the least amount of fat and sugar, I found myself falling in love with plant-based foods in a way I never had before. After all, it was by the harmonizing of plant-based foods such as fruits, vegetables, nuts, seeds, legumes, and grains that I was able to replicate my "I want a pickle!" moment over and over again.

The stars aligned, the arts won me over, and for a time, the science of my world faded into black and white, and all I could see was the blasting colors of beautiful food that tasted as good as it looked. Tiny seeds from the earth springing into picturesque produce prepared and styled with intention, suspended on the ropes of composition and lighting, gracefully spread over a canvas of a photograph, imprinting with it the flavor, texture, and mood of the story.

While pursuing my education and professional career, I met many people across a wide spectrum in society who believed vegan, plant-based, healthier cooking was too difficult, too expensive, unappealing, and time-consuming. As you can imagine, this new culinary and artistic phase in my life provided me with a fresh perspective that helped fuel the design of a resource to debunk these very myths. I like to think about these recipes as the "bait" to invite people to explore what balanced, flavorful, and wholesome plant-based eating could look like. It shouldn't stop here, though. This resource is intended to create a starting place that is as much moderate as it is effective. There's something in this book for everyone, whether for kids, parties, romantic dinners, meal prepping, it's all here.

We live in a day and age where presentation is everything. We see food before we taste it. How the food looks, how it is styled and prepared, will influence whether or not we will want it, which is why food photography is such an integral part of a cookbook's spirit. With my love of recipe creation, cooking, food styling, photography, and my credentials, it only seemed inevitable for me to create a resource of this kind that I could share with you. Here I've compiled my favorite recipes and thoughts on nutrition and plant-based cooking and put it all in a book that would look just as good sitting on your coffee table as it would be covered with flour and almond milk on your kitchen counter. This is a little piece of myself. It is my deepest hope that you will discover the beauty and elegance of creating masterpieces with clean foods and that this will be the glue that adheres you to a lifestyle rich in wholeness, health, and vitality!

Fay

FAY KAZZI, PhD, MS, RD
Author: www.TheEarthyCanvas.com

RECIPE CREATION

When I first started creating recipes, I didn't know what I was doing. It was a matter of working with whatever I had available. Trial and error were my guides, adding a little of this and a little of that until I liked what I was tasting. I remember the first time I put together a protein bar for a camping trip to Mammoth I was preparing for. I'm not a fan of the protein bars you get from the store, mostly because I didn't care much for how they taste. So I opened up my pantry of dried fruits, nuts, and nut butters and combined a little bit of everything. I'm not quite sure how it happened, but I was pleasantly surprised with how good they tasted, and with how nutrient-dense it was. You mean nutrient-dense food can still taste amazing? I guess so!

There wasn't a lot of thinking that went into creating recipes at that time. I usually based it on whatever I had in my fridge or my pantry, since going to the store just to create a new recipe that I could photograph wasn't a luxury I had at the time, and certainly wasn't anything I was getting paid for yet! Soon enough, though, as I became more skillful in my ingredient selection, I put a lot more effort into studying out flavor profiles of individual produce items. I then developed a formula for building the recipe around that one item. I felt like it came natural to me, and I began to find these individual foods inspiring with their natural beauty and flavors.

Here's a little glimpse of what a recipe being developed in my mind would look like:

"A client requests mushrooms to be highlighted in an upcoming recipe. I love working with cremini mushrooms. They are mild in flavor, meaty in texture, and have a picturesque brownish hew; this would pair beautifully with fresh herbs like thyme and parsley. These herbs can complement the mushroom's existing earthiness without overpowering it. Then we'd need a little something to elevate the mushrooms and marry these flavors, and what better than a translucent, savory roux made out of a base of reduced onions, garlic, and the juices of the sweating mushrooms? Yes, we're on to something! Now, a star component, something to be enveloped with this deliciously prepared blanket of layered savors . . . Of course, perfectly cooked pappardelle noodles. Ah, yes, this is it. I'll call it Herbed Mushroom Stroganoff!"

Can you feel me sighing with delight as I reminisce how starting with a pack of cremini mushrooms transformed into this delicious recipe? Today, I see recipe development and cooking as a form of art, an endless canvas to paint on, muse, and to enjoy.

RESOURCES & METHODS

PANTRY

For this cookbook, here are a few staple pantry items that will be convenient for you to have available when you want to throw something together:

Nuts*/seeds	Pasta	Grains	Legumes/Cans	Flours	Plant Milks
Cashews	Linguini	Quinoa	Black beans	All-purpose	Almond milk
Almonds	Pappardelle	Brown Rice	Chickpeas	almond	Hempseed milk
Walnuts	Orzo	Round Rice	Lentils	Almond meal	Coconut milk†
Pecans	Rice noodles	Basmati Rice	Roasted tomatoes	Coconut flour	
Peanuts	Vermicelli	Bulgur	Tomato paste	Tapioca flour	
Pine nuts	Gnocchi			Flaxseed meal	
Hempseeds					
Sesame seeds					
Chia seeds					

Nut butters*	Baking	Sweeteners	Oils**/fats	Seasonings	Condiments
Peanut butter	Baking soda	Maple syrup	Vegetable oil	Cumin	Apple cider vinegar
Cashew butter	Baking Powder	Agave	Grape-seed oil	Paprika	White wine vinegar
Almond butter	Vegan chocolate	Honey (optional)	Coconut oil	Cayenne	Balsamic vinegar
Tahini	chips	Coconut sugar	Olive oil	Garam masala	Ketchup
	Cocoa powder	Cane sugar	Avocado oil	Rosemary	Vegan mayonnaise
	Dark cocoa powder‡	Medjool dates	Sesame oil	Basil	Blossom water††
				Thyme	
				Cinnamon	
				Turmeric	
				Nutritional yeast	

*When referring to nuts, note, in most cases, we are using raw nuts, unless otherwise specified. For nut butters, we are always using all-natural nut butters.

†Coconut milk in this book is referring to canned coconut milk, not the coconut milk in cartons. I've used several different kinds, but the best I'd recommend for these recipes is Thai Kitchen Coconut Milk.

‡Dark cocoa powder: You'll notice the chocolate color in many of my dessert recipes is quite dark, which is my preference. That's because I like to combine regular cocoa powder with a much darker one, such as King Arthur Flour Double-Dutch Dark Cocoa Powder. You can find this on Amazon. To achieve what I have, you can go with equal parts of regular cocoa powder and a dark one.

**For the oils, you can use grape-seed oil or avocado oil in the place of any use of vegetable oil in these recipes.

††Blossom water is used for some of the Lebanese desserts in this book, such as the baklava. If you don't have a Mediterranean store nearby, you can order Orange Blossom Water on Amazon as well.

METHODS

Soaking cashews

You'll see a lot of raw cashews used in this cookbook as the base for sauces, dressings, and desserts. Cashew is the main "cream" ingredient of the plant-based world. Soaking cashews helps to enhance the creaminess we are aiming to achieve. It's ideal to soak them overnight, but you could get away with soaking them in warm water for two hours before using them in a recipe. Depending on the recipe, you will usually add some form of fluid, such as almond milk or water, and blend it with the cashew using a highspeed blender until completely smooth and creamy. If you're ever really in a rush and didn't prepare ahead, you could soak them in boiling water for at least 30 minutes and achieve similar results to having soaked them overnight. If you have extra and need to store them, drain the water, and store them in the fridge, otherwise they will go bad.

Canned coconut milk

I use quite a bit of this ingredient, and you can think about this as the "other cream" of the plant-based world. For those who might be allergic to nuts and the recipe calls for cashews, you can substitute it with canned coconut milk. There's a wide variety of full-fat coconut milk options you can get, but I would recommend the canned Thai Kitchen Coconut Milk, preferably organic, just because I find that it yields the creamiest and smoothest solid part, and it separates well from the clear liquid, which for some of the recipes we will discard. The best way to do this is to place the can in the fridge overnight, which causes the solid cream layer to harden and will allow you to easily scoop out that layer. You can use the clear fluid in a smoothie if you prefer not to waste it.

Sweeteners

The main sweetener I use in my recipes is maple syrup. I prefer this over-processed white sugar because it has a lower glycemic index and contains a good amount of minerals. It's still considered sugar to the body, but somewhat better. You will see me using dates as well. Some of my desserts are entirely sweetened with dates only. They are a fantastic, nutrient-dense sugar alternative. Some recipes will call for coconut sugar or cane sugar, but these are used sparingly in comparison with what recipes like these usually call for. There is a camp in the vegan community that is completely against honey, and one that isn't. I'm in the camp that doesn't oppose the use of honey, but not many of my recipes call for it, and you can always replace it with agave or maple syrup.

Vinegars & acids

I've been asked a few times in magazine interviews what I think is the most underutilized ingredient in our pantries, and my answer is always vinegar! I use vinegar to help sharpen the flavor of my vinaigrettes, dressings, and desserts (especially the chocolate ones!). Most of the recipes call for small amounts (1–2 tsp), but it does make a difference. Acid is an important factor in flavor balance and development. Usually you get this acidity from dairy products such as cheeses and creams in recipes. Vinegars and acids, such as lemon and lime in vegan dishes, can play an important role in replacing/mimicking these richly acidic ingredients.

Flax-egg

You're probably already familiar with the flax-egg creation. In this book, I've chosen not to use any alternative ingredients (aside from nut-based milks), such as vegan egg substitutes, meats, and cheeses. I'm not against them, but I prefer to utilize more plant-based ingredients to create versions of these since they're less processed and don't contain the unwanted chemicals and preservatives. The flax-egg is 1 Tbsp of flaxseed meal to 3 Tbsp of warm water, which equates to the adhesive properties of 1 egg. When you leave the flaxseed to sit with the water for a few minutes, it thickens and forms a sticky consistency that can be used in baking cakes or making pancakes. The idea is not to overmix your batter once you add it, which is usually the last ingredient since you don't want to weaken the flax-egg's sticky properties.

TOOLS

Cooking knives

Cooking as I know it completely changed once I invested in a good set of kitchen knives, and I'm pretty obsessed with them. It only contains three knives—one large chef knife, one medium chef knife, and one precision knife—but aside from a serrated knife for cutting bread, these are all I use. The set I have is a bit pricey for just three knives, but it is so worth it! The brand is called Global. They are Japanese blades, and yes, they can slice off a finger if you're not careful. Sharp knives are to be respected, handled with care, and regularly maintained with the use of a straightening rod. There's nothing quite so satisfying as getting through a pile of carrots with a good chef's knife versus a dull knife! Since plant-based cooking requires a lot of preparation in terms of chopping fresh produce, understanding and respecting the use of sharp, good-quality knives will go a long way in creating a long-term commitment to a plant-based lifestyle. I also recommend a large, heavy-duty cutting board. I use an industrial high-density polyethylene cutting board in my kitchen. It's heavy and bulky, but super sturdy, has a textured surface that helps hold food in place, and doesn't harbor bacteria.

High-speed blender

For creating the plant-based creams, sauces, and smoothies in this cookbook, nothing quite does the work of breaking down these more fibrous ingredients to minute particles like a good high-speed blender. I used a Vitamix to do a lot of the blending in this cookbook, and I understand it is pricey, but definitely worth the investment if you want to go fully plant-based. You can use other high-speed blenders if that's what you have. I'm only sharing with you what I know works best, but other good-quality blenders shouldn't fall too far behind in terms of a final product.

Food processor

You don't have to go too fancy with a food processor. I use a pretty cheap one I bought online. The point is the recipes requiring processing just need quick chopping and integration more than actually breaking down of the ingredients. So, whatever you already have at home should be fine. If you don't have one and don't want to break the bank, I'd recommend the Hamilton Food Processor for under $50 on Amazon.

Pots & pans

No need to overthink this area. A regular set of stainless steel pots containing a small saucepot, medium pot, and large pot will do it in the pots department for this book. For pans, you'll need a nonstick pan, and a few medium-sized stainless steel skillets will be helpful. I also recommend a cast-iron skillet, which you'll need for some of the recipes.

Measuring equipment

A basic set of measuring cups and spoons will do it for this book based on the U.S. customary units of measurement, e.g., cup (C), pound (lb), tablespoon (Tbsp), ounce (oz), etc.

Brea

kfast

ORANGE-ZESTED OAT WAFFLES & CHOCOLATE MAPLE SYRUP

GLUTEN FREE

MAKES

···《 4 》···

WAFFLES

Let's take this wide-eyed childhood favorite of ours and douse it with a serving of healthy, for an irresistible and guilt-free twist. Switch up the usual wheat flour with oat flour that is gluten free, easy on the gut, and even protective against heart disease. Some of the benefits, per studies of dietary oats, include its plasma cholesterol-lowering effects, anti-inflammatory and antioxidant effects, and maintenance of arterial function. Craving chocolate syrup, but not feeling too good about empty calories? Try making it yourself with some organic cocoa powder, maple syrup, and a little coconut oil. Yes, good-looking food can do a body good!

INGREDIENTS

Batter
1 ½ C oat flour
¾ C almond milk
¼ C macadamia nuts, ground
3 Tbsp coconut oil
2 flax-eggs (2 Tbsp of ground flaxseed + 6 Tbsp warm water)
1 Tbsp maple syrup
2 tsp baking powder
1 tsp orange zest
½ tsp vanilla extract
¼ tsp salt

Chocolate Maple Syrup
3 Tbsp maple syrup
3 Tbsp coconut oil
1 Tbsp dark cocoa powder

Toppings
Fresh strawberries
Coconut cream, optional
Powder sugar
Orange zest

DIRECTIONS

1. Mix in all dry ingredients first, then set aside. Mix all wet ingredients, then add to dry ingredients. Mix thoroughly.

2. For the flax-eggs, mix together until thickened. Incorporate into your batter.

3. Divide into 4 parts. Use each part for one waffle, with your waffle maker.

4. For the chocolate maple syrup, microwave coconut oil with maple syrup, and mix well. Then add cocoa powder and mix thoroughly. Drizzle on to waffles with toppings as desired. Enjoy!

COCONUT-CRUSTED FRENCH TOAST FINGERS

SERVES

··· « 2 ～ 4 » ···

I had a sudden urge for French toast one morning and challenged myself to create a vegan version. But what is French toast without eggs, you might think? Well, I figured if we covered it with a tasty enough batter and fused it in crispy coconut, that you might not even notice it was missing! But then, I was pleasantly surprised to find it not only looked incredible, but tasted *better* than any other French toast I have ever had. You might say, "Well, eggs have B-12, though." And I'll just say, "No worries, so does nutritional yeast!"

INGREDIENTS

12-inch whole-wheat French bread
1 C almond milk
¼ C shredded coconut
2 Tbsp flour
2 Tbsp maple syrup
1 Tbsp canola oil
2 tsp nutritional yeast
1 tsp cinnamon
¼ tsp salt
¼ tsp vanilla extract

Toppings
Fruit of your choice
Maple syrup
Powdered sugar

DIRECTIONS

1. Cut 1-inch slices of French bread. Cut each slice into 2–3 strips.

2. Take the almond milk and whisk with the flour, maple syrup, nutritional yeast, cinnamon, salt, and vanilla extract until fully incorporated.

3. Oil a nonstick pan and set to medium heat. Place coconut on a plate. Soak the strips in your mix and roll on to the coconut, then place in your hot pan. Cook each side in the pan until golden brown and crispy, about 2 minutes each side.

4. Let cool on a metal rack. Serve with maple syrup and fruit of choice. Enjoy!

BLUEBERRY OATMEAL

MAKES
···« *2 Bowls* »···

This is my husband's go-to breakfast on slower mornings when he's not in a rush. He feels it sets him up to have a great day! This is also a good breakfast option for individuals who have stomach sensitivities, which he has to deal with from time to time. It's easy to digest and still manages to be very comforting and delicious. Oats are high in complex carbohydrates and soluble fibers, which means they keep you feeling full longer and can even help to control cholesterol. Also, blueberries are high in antioxidants, which are important to have for that early morning immune boost we all want!

INGREDIENTS

2 ½ C almond milk or water
1 ½ C rolled oats
1 Tbsp maple syrup
½ tsp vanilla extract
½ C frozen blueberries

Top with
Fresh blueberries
Shaved almonds

DIRECTIONS

1. Place your almond milk or water in a pot and bring to a boil. Once boiling, add the oats and remaining ingredients, except for the frozen blueberries. Set to a simmer, and cook for 7–10 minutes, until softened. For a creamier porridge, opt for the almond milk.

2. Once cooked, pour into bowls, and lightly mix in your frozen blueberries. They will bleed nicely and give a pretty hue to your oatmeal. If you cook it directly with the blueberries, your oatmeal will turn a bluish-gray and may not look as appetizing.

3. Top with fresh blueberries and your shaved almonds. Enjoy!

COCONUT RICE PUDDING WITH MANGO

SERVES

···« 6 »···

When I was going to school, my mom used to make large batches of rice pudding and put them in little cups and bowls stored in the fridge as a quick breakfast and snack option for us growing teens. She used to add pineapple chunks to it. Here is a play on this school-time classic using mango instead. This is fantastic since it is 100% plant-based, contains no dairy, but still is so creamy thanks to the starchiness of round rice combined with the buttery goodness of coconut milk. This could be a dessert or breakfast option. Normally a batch of rice pudding like this would call for double or triple the amount of sugar, but we're only using a little over ⅓ of a cup. This rice pudding holds well in the fridge and is also a fun, dairy-free snack option that kids will love!

INGREDIENTS

1 ¼ C rice
4 C almond milk
3 C water
1 can coconut milk
⅓ C + 1 Tbsp cane sugar
½ tsp vanilla extract
¼ tsp salt
A few dashes of cinnamon

Toppings

Shredded coconut
Crushed pistachio
Mango

DIRECTIONS

1. In a large pot, add the water and the rice first, and bring to a boil. Once boiling, set heat to low-medium and continue to boil for 10 minutes. Stir frequently.

2. Now add the almond milk. Once boiling again, allow to continue for another 10 minutes, stirring frequently.

3. Now add the coconut milk, sugar, and remaining ingredients. Bring again to a boil, and then let simmer for about 10–15 minutes while stirring frequently. You will notice halfway through that the mixture will begin to thicken.

4. Once done, the mixture should be soft and creamy. Turn off heat. You can serve it hot or let it cool down and allow to chill in the fridge, whichever you prefer. I personally prefer it chilled. Enjoy!

APPLE CINNAMON OATMEAL

MAKES
··« 2 Bowls »··

As much as I enjoy blueberry oatmeal, my all-time favorite way to fix oatmeal is with fresh apples and lots of cinnamon. It is so yummy! I love how creamy oatmeal can become when cooked just perfectly. I know it's a simple and seemingly peasant type of breakfast to rave about, but it always manages to hit the spot and be the best hardy option to kick-start my day. Although this recipe has cooked apple in the oatmeal, I still like to top it with a generous portion of freshly cut apple and a few extra dashes of cinnamon. Yum!

INGREDIENTS

2 ½ C almond milk or water

1 ½ C rolled oats

1 Tbsp maple syrup

½ tsp vanilla extract

¼ tsp cinnamon

1 Fuji or honeycrisp apple,
    chopped

Top with

Fresh apple pieces

Shaved almonds

A few dashes of cinnamon

DIRECTIONS

1. Place your almond milk or water in a pot and bring to a boil. Once boiling, add the oats and remaining ingredients. Set to a simmer for about 7–10 minutes, stirring occasionally. Wait to add the chopped apples until 2 3 minutes before turning off the heat. For a creamier porridge, opt for the almond milk.

2. Once cooked, pour into bowls. Top with your fresh apple pieces, shaved almonds, and a few dashes of cinnamon. Enjoy!

BLUEBERRY & TURMERIC CHIA SEED PUDDING

MAKES

…« 2~3 Cups »…

This might sound like a daring chia seed pudding, but after just a few bites, you'll find it to be deliciously pleasant as a breakfast option that is packed full of dietary benefits. Blueberry and turmeric are loaded with antioxidant and anti-inflammatory properties. They are both considered "beauty foods" and improve skin's appearance by increasing blood circulation. Chia seeds are a great source of essential fats and protein. This pudding is so easy to put together and is a fun breakfast option to kick-start your day with a burst of energy!

INGREDIENTS

Turmeric layer
1 C almond milk
¼ C white chia seeds
1 Tbsp maple syrup
2 Tbsp peanut butter
¼ tsp vanilla extract

Blueberry layer
¾ C almond milk
½ C blueberries, frozen
¼ C white chia seeds
1 Tbsp maple syrup
¼ vanilla extract

Top with
Chia seeds
Choice of nuts

DIRECTIONS

1. For the turmeric layer, warm almond milk in microwave for 30 seconds. Mix all ingredients for 2–3 minutes, until it begins to thicken. Set aside.

2. For the blueberry layer, throw blueberries and almond milk into a Vitamix or high-speed blender, and blend until completely smooth. Add remaining ingredients, and mix until thickened.

3. Store in the fridge in individual Tupperware (or Mason jars), and chill for 1–2 hours.

4. Layer as desired in a long glass and top with chia seeds or nuts of your preference. Enjoy!

BANANA BREAD

MAKES

···« 2 4x8—inch Pans »···

Believe it or not, this was the hardest recipe to get right! Since we are not using eggs, the temperature and consistency are challenging to get right when baking a vegan bread-cake that is denser due to the banana and nuts, and often it flattens shortly after rising. I'm so thankful this recipe worked out (mostly due to the flax-egg), and I just love how light and fluffy it turned out! I personally will dollop a generous portion of all-natural peanut butter and spread it all over a thick slice. Wonderful to have for a quick breakfast with some fresh fruit. So good!

INGREDIENTS

Dry

2 C organic flour
⅓ C crushed walnuts
4 ½ tsp baking powder
½ C organic cane sugar
2 Tbsp flaxseed meal
1 tsp cinnamon
½ tsp salt

Wet

1 very ripe banana
1 C almond milk
¼ C canola oil
6 Tbsp water
1 tsp champagne vinegar
½ tsp vanilla extract

DIRECTIONS

1. Take the 6 Tbsp of warm water and place in a small saucepan with the flaxseed. Set to medium heat, and stir for 2–3 minutes, or until thickened to make your flax-eggs. Cover and set aside to cool.

2. Mash the banana, then place in a small bowl with remaining wet ingredients. Mix thoroughly.

3. Place dry ingredients in a larger bowl and mix. Pour the wet ingredients and mix with the dry ingredients. When partially mixed, add the flax-egg mixture, and mix just until incorporated. Do not overmix the batter.

4. Lightly oil your pans. Divide batter and pour into your pans.

5. Set your oven to 375 degrees and bake for 25–30 minutes. Then set to 350 and bake for another 10–15 minutes. Test cake by putting a knife in the center to the bottom. If it pulls out clean it is ready. If not, give it 3–5 more minutes. Enjoy!

STRAWBERRY CHIA SEED PUDDING

SERVES

···《 4 》···

One of my favorite breakfast options to have is chia seed pudding. It takes about five minutes to prep with your favorite milk substitute. Don't let these tiny seeds deceive you, "chia" means strength, and for a good reason. Chia seeds are known to contain substantial amounts of omega-3 fatty acids, carbohydrates, protein, fiber, antioxidants, and calcium. A one-ounce portion contains 11 grams of fiber, 4 grams of protein, and 9 grams of fat (5g of which are omega-3s!). I love having chia seed pudding with fresh strawberries, but you can always substitute with other berries and add bananas!

INGREDIENTS

Chia seed pudding
1 C white chia seeds
5 C of almond milk
3 Tbsp maple syrup, or honey
2 Tbsp shredded coconut
2 Tbsp crushed walnuts
1 tsp vanilla extract
1 tsp orange blossom
   water (optional)

Strawberry sauce
1 C fresh strawberries
3 Tbsp maple syrup
1 Tbsp water
1 Tbsp lemon
¼ tsp champagne vinegar

Topping
Fresh strawberry slices

DIRECTIONS

1. Mix contents of chia seed pudding. After mixing for 1 minute, microwave for about 40–50 seconds. Mix again for another minute or so. You'll notice the mix will already begin to thicken. Place in a container with a lid, and let it chill overnight.

2. Strawberry sauce: Use a food processor and pulse ingredients for saucy consistency. (Add water if you'd like it thinner.)

3. Place in glass jars, layer, and style with your choice of fresh berries. Add strawberry sauce on top of the pudding, or mix in. Enjoy!

CHOCOLATE-ORANGE PROTEIN BARS

MAKES
···« 20~25 2x3—inch Bars »···

USE A SMALL BAKING SHEET

I was never really a fan of packaged energy bars and just felt many of them were too sweet, had too many preservatives, and were not as nutrient-dense as they could be. So I decided to make my own, and I absolutely love them! Not too long ago, I took a little Tupperware full of these to a twelve-mile hiking adventure out in Mammoth, California. They were such a fun and tasty treat to munch on! Oats combined with dates and nuts act as complex carbohydrates that provide a long-acting sugar supply to the blood. Such a great option to keep you going on your physically demanding days!

INGREDIENTS

Dry
2 ½ C oat flour
2 C almond flour
1 ½ C chia seed
3 Tbsp dark cocoa powder
1 Tbsp tapioca powder
¼ C shredded coconut

Wet
½ C all-natural cashew butter
½ C all-natural peanut butter
¾ C date paste
½ C almond milk
3 Tbsp honey (increases
　sweetness), as desired
2 Tbsp coconut butter
1 tsp orange zest
½ tsp vanilla extract

DIRECTIONS

1. Incorporate all dry ingredients in the bowl. Mix.

2. Add all wet ingredients to dry ingredients, adding date paste, almond milk, and honey last. Use your hands to fully incorporate all the ingredients.

3. Place parchment paper on the tray, and press your mix into the tray. Refrigerate for a few hours, then cut out bars. Store in the fridge. Enjoy!

NUTTY BREAKFAST BARS

MAKES
···《 20~25 1.5x3–inch Bars 》···

USE A 9X12-INCH PYREX OR BAKING TRAY

If you're like me and are always on the go, then these breakfast bars will be sure to satisfy your hunger and provide you with all the balanced, high-energy nutrients you need for your busy days! Peanuts, pecans, and cashews, all of which are high in protein and rich in healthy fats. Plant-based fats are highly necessary for cell function and hormonal production. Nuts are also a good source of dietary fiber and have a wide range of vitamins, such as B and E vitamins. These could also be a great "healthy dessert" option for toddlers and kids. They look like mini ice cream bars and are best right out of the freezer.

INGREDIENTS

Crust
2 packs graham crackers
   (8–9 crackers/pack)
1 ½ C pecans
5–6 Tbsp almond milk
3 Tbsp coconut oil
¼ tsp salt

Filling
1 can coconut milk, cream
   part only
1 C all-natural peanut butter
1 C all-natural cashew butter
8–9 Medjool dates
2 Tbsp lemon juice
⅓ C maple syrup
3 tsp lemon zest
1 Tbsp tapioca starch in 3 Tbsp
   hot water
1 ½ C frozen strawberries
¼ tsp vanilla extract

Chocolate drizzle
1 Tbsp coconut oil
1 Tbsp maple syrup
1 ½ tsp cocoa powder
1 small bag baby
   pretzels (optional)

DIRECTIONS

1. Soak the dates in warm water for about 10 minutes

2. Place graham crackers into a food processor until powdered. Then do the same with the pecans.

3. Mix graham crackers and pecans with almond milk, salt, and coconut oil. Use your hands to ensure the coconut oil is worked into the crust. Press into a tray.

4. For the filling, begin by blending the coconut milk, peanut butter, cashew butter, and dates in the food processor until smooth. Then add lemon juice, maple syrup, vanilla extract, and zest, and blend.

5. Mix the tapioca powder in the 3 Tbsp of warm-hot water, until thickened. Add to the mixture.

6. Remove 2 C from the mixture. Set aside. Then pour the remaining mixture on top of the crust and spread evenly.

7. For the strawberry layer, run the food processor with the frozen strawberries and 2 C of mixture until smooth. Add this as the top layer of your bars. Spread evenly and create swirls using a toothpick.

8. Optional step: Press baby pretzels into the top layer.

9. For the chocolate drizzle, place coconut oil in the microwave for about 20–25 seconds. Mix with maple syrup and cocoa powder, should drizzle nicely.

10. Place in the freezer overnight, and cut the next day into bars. Store in an airtight Tupperware in the freezer. Allow to thaw for a few minutes before eating. Enjoy!

SAVORY WAFFLES & BEET HUMMUS

SERVES

···« 4 »···

At first sight, you might think this is some sort of sweet, raspberry topping on maple syrup flavored waffles, but after one bite, you'll discover it's savory! Of course, I had to throw in some yellow tomatoes to add a whimsical twist to this already adventurous dish. But don't be fooled, this plate is loaded with vitamins, nutrients, and protein! Beets are a superfood that is high in vitamin C, fiber, and essential minerals. This immune-boosting food has also been shown to lower blood pressure, fight inflammation, and has detoxifying and anticancer properties. This one's sure to win your heart in more ways than one!

INGREDIENTS

Waffles

Dry
2 C flour
1 tsp baking soda
½ tsp salt
A few dashes black pepper

Wet
1 C unsweetened almond milk
⅓ C vegetable stock
⅓ C cashews soaked 2 hours
1 flax-egg (1 Tbsp flaxseed meal +
   3 Tbsp hot water)
2 Tbsp vegetable oil
2 Tbsp green onion, minced
1 Tbsp maple syrup
1 tsp fresh thyme, minced

Beet hummus
1 medium-sized beet
2 cans garbanzo beans, strained
¼–½ C water (depending on
   desired consistency)
Juice of one lemon
¼ C tahini
2–3 cloves of garlic
½–1 tsp salt

Serve with yellow tomatoes

DIRECTIONS

1. For the waffles, in a bowl, mix the dry ingredients. Set aside.

2. For the flax-egg, place the 3 Tbsp of water in a small cup, then microwave for 25–30 seconds. Mix with the flaxseed meal and set aside.

3. Strain the soaked cashews and place in a food processor with the almond milk and vegetable stock. Process until smooth and creamy. Place in a separate bowl, and add remaining wet ingredients, except the flax-egg. Once incorporated, mix with the dry ingredients. Then add the flax-egg. Mix until fully incorporated.

4. Lightly oil spray your waffle maker and place about half a cup or more of the batter. Cook until desired browning is reached.

5. For the beet hummus, peel your beet, cut into large chunks, and steam for 25–30 minutes, until cooked through. Set aside to cool.

6. Throw your strained garbanzo beans, tahini, garlic, lemon juice, water, and salt in a Vitamix or high-speed blender. Blend until smooth. Then add about half of the steamed beets or more, depending on how dark of a pink you would like. Dollop a generous portion on to your waffles. Garnish with fresh thyme and serve with yellow tomatoes. Enjoy!

TOFU SCRAMBLE BREAKFAST BURRITOS

SERVES
··· « 4 ～ 6 » ···

I love working with tortillas because you can pack a beautiful variety of healthy and tasty layers, roll it all up, and go! You can use this as a meal prep option and freeze several for your on-the-go days. Wrap in foil, and place in a plastic bag in the freezer, then microwave for two minutes when ready to eat. Black beans are high in protein and minerals, such as calcium and magnesium. Yams contain good amounts of vitamin C and A—the darker the orange color, the higher these vitamins are! I'm such a fan of lacinato kale because it's loaded with iron and fiber. This breakfast burrito is a fabulous nutrient- and energy-dense option to keep the on-the-goer powered up for the whole day!

INGREDIENTS

3–4 medium-sized yams
1 bunch lacinato kale
2 cans black beans
1 medium red onion
1 block tofu
2 ripe avocados
Juice of ½ a lemon
1 ½ Tbsp vegetable oil

Seasonings

½ tsp turmeric
2 tsp nutritional yeast
½ tsp garlic powder
1 ½ tsp salt
¼ tsp black pepper

Tortilla

Whole wheat or white

DIRECTIONS

1. Start with yams. Cut up into small cubes, and place in a large bowl. Add 1 Tbsp vegetable oil, 1 tsp of salt, and a little black pepper, with a few dashes of garlic powder. Pop in the oven at 350 degrees for 30 minutes. Then broil for 5–7 minutes. Remove from oven.

2. Dice the onion. Cook on stove with ½ Tbsp vegetable oil until golden. Drain the beans and add in. Cook for 10–15 minutes. Add salt and black pepper, to taste. Set aside to cool, then mash the beans and onion with a potato masher.

3. Drain the tofu, then crumble and place in a lightly oiled pan on medium heat. Add turmeric, nutritional yeast, and salt and pepper, to taste. Set aside.

4. You can mash the avocados or slice them. Add a little lemon and garlic powder, and set aside.

5. Massage kale, and cut up strips. Take warmed tortilla, spread on a layer of beans. Then top with yams, tofu scramble, avocado, and kale. Wrap, slice, and serve! Enjoy!

Entr

ées

PASTA MARINARA WITH WILTED SPINACH

SERVES

···《 4 》···

Marinara sauce done right with the perfect al dente pasta and hints of fresh basil is one of the most effortlessly comforting foods you can indulge in. I love incorporating dark greens in my more carbohydrate-dense dishes for an extra boost of fiber and nutrients. Here, I added some beautifully wilted spinach. Nutrition plug: Always remember to add a squeeze of lemon to your dark greens, as the vitamin C improves the absorption of iron in the greens. The spinach is subtle enough not to overpower the pasta, but perfectly apparent to produce a beautiful contrast to the vibrantly red tomatoes. This dish is truly your "Italy in a bowl" experience!

INGREDIENTS

1 lb box linguine pasta

Pasta sauce
2 C canned tomato chunks
  + ½ C water
1 C cherry tomatoes, sliced in two
1 red onion, finely chopped
3–4 cloves of garlic, minced
1 Tbsp vegetable oil
2 tsp olive oil
1 tsp of sugar
1 tsp of salt
1 tsp of dried basil
½ tsp oregano
¼ tsp black pepper
A few dashes of cayenne pepper
Fresh basil leaves

Roasted tomatoes on vine
Cluster of small tomatoes on vine
2 tsp olive oil
Salt and pepper, to taste

Spinach
3–4 C raw spinach
1 Tbsp lemon juice
1 Tbsp vegetable oil
Salt and pepper, to taste

DIRECTIONS

1. Cook pasta according to directions. Add a tsp of oil and a few dashes of salt into the water used to cook the pasta. When done, rinse under cool water to stop the cooking process. Set aside.

2. Sauté chopped onion in 1 Tbsp of vegetable oil. Stir for 2 minutes or so, until transparency occurs. Add garlic, followed by cherry tomatoes. After sautéing, add tomato chunks. Stir for a few minutes, then add sugar, salt, basil, oregano, and peppers. Stir until well incorporated. Let this boil and then set to a simmer for about 10 minutes. Finally, add 2 tsp of olive oil and chopped fresh basil leaves.

3. For the roasted tomatoes on vine, place 1 Tbsp olive oil in a small bowl with salt and pepper, to taste. Use a cooking brush to dab directly on to tomatoes. Place in the oven and set to bake for 10 minutes at 350 degrees. Then set to broil for 5 minutes. Remove from oven and set aside to cool.

4. For the wilted spinach, lightly oil a pan on heat. Add spinach with lemon juice and salt and pepper, to taste. Once wilted, remove from heat. Style as desired. Enjoy!

HERBED MUSHROOM STROGANOFF

SERVES

···« 4 »···

Where do I begin with how magnificent this dish is! Beautifully cooked mushrooms infused with melted onions, simmered down in a luxurious bath of vegetable stock, reduced to a perfectly translucent roux, tangled in deliciously al dente pappardelle noodles. *Faint.* The herbs in this dish balance and compliment the umami flavors of the mushrooms and add a nutritional twist to the plate. Thyme is high in vitamins A and C and has been shown to treat stomach aches, colds, and some digestive disorders. Parsley is high in antioxidants, improves digestion, and even has antibacterial properties. OK, we get it, it looks and sounds amazing *and* it's good for you!

INGREDIENTS

3 ½ C vegetable stock
¾ C unsweetened almond milk
½ lb (8 oz) pappardelle noodles
1 large yellow onion, chopped
2 ½ Tbsp flour
½ lb (8 oz) cremini mushrooms, sliced
½ C parsley, chopped
3 cloves of garlic, minced
2 Tbsp vegetable oil
2 tsp fresh thyme, minced
1 tsp salt (add more as desired)
¼ tsp black pepper

DIRECTIONS

1. Sauté onions on medium-high heat in a large pot with 1 Tbsp of oil, until golden and transparent (4–6 minutes). Add the sliced mushrooms and cook for another 5 minutes or so, until the water has seeped out.

2. Add your minced garlic and thyme, along with another Tbsp of oil. Cook for a few minutes. Then add the flour and mix until mushrooms and onion are well coated. Add vegetable stock and almond milk. Bring to a boil.

3. Once boiling, add the noodles and cook with lid off for 8–10 minutes, until al dente. During this time, add your salt and black pepper. Feel free to add more or less according to your taste.

4. Once done, mix in half of your parsley. Then garnish with the rest. Serve immediately. If there are leftovers, place in the fridge in an airtight container. Can hold up to 3–5 days. Enjoy!

CREAMY MACARONI & CHEESE

SERVES

··· « 6 » ···

Among all my recipes, this has to be my crowd favorite. It's quite a showstopper because it really does taste, feel, and look like traditional macaroni and cheese, and even better. Thanks to the power of the incredible cashews, we're able harness the luxury of creaminess without compromising on the dish's health benefits. When your macaroni elbows are doused in disguised veggies and nuts, it takes the satisfaction level and flavor profile to a whole new level. I hope you enjoy my plant-based twist on this much loved and timeless classic!

INGREDIENTS

16 oz dried elbow macaroni

2 medium golden potatoes, peeled, cut into chunks

2 medium carrots, cut into chunks

1 white onion, cut into chunks

1 C water (used to cook vegetables)

¾ C raw cashews, soaked for 1–2 hours

½ C vegetable stock

2 Medjool dates

2 Tbsp nutritional yeast

1 Tbsp vegetable oil

1 Tbsp lemon juice

½ Tbsp white wine vinegar

2 garlic cloves

½ tsp fresh ginger, chopped

1 ½ tsp salt

¼ tsp paprika

A few dashes of cayenne pepper

Toppings

Cayenne pepper

Fresh parsley

DIRECTIONS

1. Follow instructions on your macaroni package. When done, strain with cold water to stop the cooking process. Add a little oil and mix to prevent sticking. Set aside.

2. Throw chunks of potato, carrots, and onion in boiling water for 10–15 minutes, until cooked through. Strain veggies (keep water it was boiled in).

3. Place veggies in Vitamix or high-speed blender with raw cashews, vegetable stock, and remaining ingredients. Add 1 C of the water you cooked the veggies with. If too thick, add a bit more. Blend thoroughly, until creamy consistency is created (will resemble the movement of melted chocolate).

4. Pour over pasta, mix, and add a dash of cayenne and some chopped fresh parsley. Enjoy!

AVOCADO PESTO FETTUCCINE

SERVES

··· « 4 » ···

Everyone loves a good pesto dish, but how about a pesto dish that is as creamy as fettuccine Alfredo? Well, thanks to the incredible avocado, this plate is the combination of the best of both worlds, *and* it's lower in calories and higher in nutrients! Avocados are incredibly nutritious and high in essential fats and omega-3s. Let's face it, just eating an avocado plain with a little pepper and salt is exciting, so this might blow your mind a little.

INGREDIENTS

1 box linguine or fettuccine
1 Tbsp vegetable oil

Sauce

2 C fresh basil
2 ripe medium-sized avocados
Handful of pine nuts
¾ C water
2 pitted Medjool dates
2 Tbsp olive oil
3 cloves garlic
1 Tbsp white wine vinegar
1 ½ tsp sea salt
¼ tsp black pepper

Roasted veggies

1 bunch Asparagus
3 vines of cherry tomatoes
1 tsp vegetable oil
¼ tsp sea salt
A few dashes black pepper

Topping

Handful of sun-dried
   tomatoes, julienned
Fresh basil leaves
Toasted pine nuts

DIRECTIONS

1. Follow the directions of your pasta. When done, done run under cold water, then add a little oil to prevent sticking.

2. For the veggies, chop off the lighter ends of the asparagus, then slice 2-inch pieces. Marinate two-inch pieces with salt, pepper, and vegetable oil. Leaving the tomatoes whole, repeat the same process. Line a baking tray with parchment paper or foil. Place tomatoes on one end and the asparagus on the other. Set oven to 350 degrees and bake for 10 minutes. Then set to broil for 5 minutes.

3. For the pesto, place all ingredients in a food processor. Blend until semi-smooth and partly grainy.

4. In a large bowl, mix the pasta with the asparagus. Pour in the sauce and lightly toss. Top with the roasted tomatoes. Garnish with sun-dried tomatoes, fresh basil, and toasted pine nuts. Enjoy!

EGGPLANT FETTUCCINE ALFREDO

SERVES

··· « 4 » ···

Similar to the previous recipe, by simply harnessing the plant-based fats from raw cashews, we are again able to create the likeness of the luxurious creaminess of fettuccine Alfredo, usually made with unforgivingly high amounts of cream and butter. With just the right flavors and ingredients, you will be surprised how "buttery" this pasta can become. I wanted to pair it with something unique, yet humble enough not to overpower the pasta's simplicity. These crispy eggplant chips created just the perfect texture contrast I was looking for. Plant-based, creamy, and frivolously delicious. Yes please!

INGREDIENTS

1 box fettuccine

Alfredo
1 C of raw cashews (soaked 1–2 hours)
½ C unsweetened almond milk
½ C water (add more later if too thick)
2 Tbsp olive oil
1 medium golden potato, steamed
Juice of ½ lemon
2–3 cloves of garlic
1 stem of fresh rosemary
1 tsp salt (add more as desired)
¼ tsp lemon zest
¼ tsp black pepper

Roasted eggplant
2 medium-sized eggplants
1 Tbsp olive oil
½ C raw cashews (not soaked)
½ tsp sea salt
1 stem of rosemary
½ tsp of lemon zest
A few dashes of cracked black pepper

Topping
Fresh basil
Green onion, diced
Cracked pepper

DIRECTIONS

1. Follow directions for fettuccine. Once done, rinse under cold water and add a little vegetable oil to prevent sticking.

2. For the sauce, Vitamix or high-speed blend soaked cashews, potato, olive oil, almond milk, lemon juice, zest, garlic, and bits of the rosemary until smooth consistency (add water if too thick).

3. Optional: Cook fettuccine sauce for 5 minutes if you prefer a hot dish.

4. For the roasted eggplant, slice eggplants in half, then cut roughly ¼-inch slices. Marinate with olive oil, crushed garlic and rosemary, crushed cashews (you can use a coffee grinder until you get a grainy consistency), lemon zest, salt, and black pepper.

5. Line a tray with parchment paper. Spread eggplant. Bake for 10–15 minutes at 350 degrees. Then broil for 5–10 minutes. Watch closely to prevent burning. Leave in the oven for a few more minutes for increased crispiness.

6. Mix in sauce with fettuccine. Add crispy roasted eggplant last. Garnish with diced green onion, fresh basil, and cracked pepper. Enjoy!

ARTICHOKE POTPIE

SERVES

···≪ 4 ≫···

4 4X2-INCH RAMEKINS

This is one of the recipes that comes from the warmest part of my heart. If you're looking to create a memorable and luxurious experience, then this is the ace up your sleeve. This recipe looks complicated, but it is actually very easy and fun to put together. There are so many incredibly savory layers to this potpie, from the flaky herbed crust to the gravy immersed veggies. It has just the perfect amount of resistance at the beginning of each bite, followed by an effortless marrying of consistencies into one flawless morsel. From my heart to your plate. Enjoy!

INGREDIENTS

Crust
2 C flour
3 Tbsp vegetable shortening
4 Tbsp vegetable oil
4 Tbsp water
1 tsp salt
1 tsp coconut sugar
½ tsp oregano
A stem of fresh thyme, minced

Sauce
1 C vegetable stock
1 C water
¾ C raw cashews, soaked 2 hours
2 Tbsp flour
2 tsp nutritional yeast
2 cloves of garlic
1 ½ tsp salt
¼ tsp black pepper
¼ tsp oregano
¼ tsp basil
A few dashes of cayenne

Vegetables
2 C cremini mushroom, chopped
1 C artichoke hearts, chopped
1 C carrots, chopped
1 C peas
1 red onion, diced
1 Tbsp vegetable oil

DIRECTIONS

1. For the crust, mix dry ingredients in a bowl. Then incorporate wet ingredients. Start using your hands to fully incorporate oils into the dough. Slowly add water one tsp at a time. Work and press dough until you have one mound and there is no longer any loose flour. Cover with plastic wrap, and place in the fridge for about 30 minutes.

2. While waiting, start prepping sauce and veggies. Blend all ingredients for the sauce in a food processor, Vitamix or high-speed blender until smooth and creamy.

3. Sauté vegetables with oil for about 5 minutes over medium-high heat in a pot. Add sauce into the vegetable pot and cook until it boils. Then turn off heat and cover with the lid while you prep your baking bowls.

4. Remove dough from fridge and cut into 4 parts. Then split each again so you have 8 equal parts. Dust a little flour on your counter and roll each part into a thin layer. Cut out about a 6-inch circle for the base, and fold into your baking cup. With the remaining piece, cut out about a 5-inch circle for the top. Repeat for the remaining pieces. When ready, scoop in veggie stew. Cover with the 5-inch top, and "cup" the edges inwards to create a small dome. Repeat for the remaining pieces. With any remaining dough you can cut out leaves or any other form of decor. Using a brush, lightly oil the dough layer when finished.

5. Place in the oven at 350 degrees for about 25–30 minutes. Then set to broil for 5 minutes to get that golden brown hue. Top with fresh thyme. Enjoy!

PESTO GNOCCHI WITH ROASTED VEGGIES

SERVES

···« 3 ⁓ 4 »···

Pesto originated in Genoa, Italy. The traditional base includes crushed garlic, pine nuts, basil leaves, coarse salt, cheese, and olive oil. This recipe is a play on the most prominent flavors of pesto, without the use of dairy, and definitely less oil. Gnocchi is made out of flour and potato, so it's quite filling, and a little goes a long way. I wanted to balance these Italian flavors with the sweet earthiness of baby vine tomatoes, pearl onions, and cremini, which also added some extra fiber and nutrients. Deliciously aromatic, unapologetically Italian, this dish comes with subtle side smiles with every bite.

INGREDIENTS

Gnocchi
16 oz pack gnocchi
5 quarts water
2–3 Tbsp salt

Pesto
2 C fresh basil
½ C pine nuts
3 cloves garlic
3 Tbsp olive oil
½ C water (add more for
    thinner consistency)
2 tsp nutritional yeast
1 tsp salt (add more as desired)
¼ tsp black pepper

Veggies
Tomatoes on vine
Cremini mushrooms
Pearl onions
Asparagus (optional)

Marinade for veggies
1 Tbsp balsamic vinegar
2 tsp olive oil
¼ tsp salt
¼ tsp black pepper

Garnish
Fresh basil leaves
Sun-dried tomatoes

DIRECTIONS

1. Follow the directions on your gnocchi packet, otherwise, boil about 5 quarts of water in a large pot with 2–3 Tbsp salt. Add gnocchi, let boil for about 10 minutes, or until gnocchi floats to the top. Strain and rinse with cold water. Set aside.

2. Run pesto ingredients in a food processor until well incorporated (add more or less water for desired consistency).

3. Lightly toss gnocchi with pesto.

4. For the veggies, marinate and spread evenly on a tray. Place in the oven at 375 degrees and bake for 15–20 minutes. Then broil for 5 minutes.

5. Serve veggies next to gnocchi with fresh basil leaves and sun-dried tomatoes. Enjoy!

CHEESY NO-CHEESE VEGGIE PIZZA

MAKES

···« 2 Medium—Sized Pizzas »···

We all love pizza, and one of the main things we love most about it is the *cheese*. As you can imagine, it's no easy task trying to replicate this incredible gastronomic experience using plant sources, but you can get very close! I was able to achieve this by combining cashews with tapioca! Tapioca is a starch that is used as a thickening agent, and with the right measurements it can get sticky and gummy, just like melted cheese! Believe it or not, there's also some nutritional perks to tapioca, and it's been found to promote cell growth and even build stronger bones. With a homemade crust and lots of veggie toppings, this pizza right here is simply out of this world.

INGREDIENTS

Crust
¼ oz yeast
¾ C warm water
2 Tbsp olive oil
1 Tbsp sugar
1 tsp salt
2 C flour

Vegan cheese
½ C raw cashew, soaked, 1 hour
1 ½ C water
3 ½ Tbsp tapioca
2 Tbsp nutritional yeast
1 Tbsp lemon juice
1 tsp onion powder
1 tsp garlic powder
½ tsp salt
A few dashes of black pepper

Sauce
Pizza or marinara sauce

Veggie toppings
White onion
Cherry tomatoes
Cremini mushrooms
Fresh basil

DIRECTIONS

1. In a bowl, place the warm water. Sprinkle yeast and leave until foamy, about 5 minutes. Whisk oil, sugar, and salt into your mixture. Then add the flour. Stir using your hands until a sticky dough forms. Transfer to another bowl that has been lightly oiled. Then lightly oil the top of the dough. Cover the bowl with plastic wrap and let rise for one hour.

2. While your dough is rising, prepare your vegan cheese. Place all the ingredients in a Vitamix or high-speed blender, and blend until smooth. Pour into a small pot and place over medium-high heat. Mix until thickened and sticky, about 10 minutes. Cover with lid.

3. Once dough has risen, split into two pieces (one for each pizza). Dust flour onto a clean surface and begin to knead and roll out your dough until the desired thickness of the pizza dough is created. Add flour as you go if it's too sticky.

4. Dust some cornmeal and a little flour onto a pan or baking stone, and form your pizza crust on it. Spread sauce onto the surface. Using a spoon, dollop your vegan cheese until partially covering the surface. Then top with veggies.

5. Set oven to 400 degrees. Bake your pizza for 10–15 minutes, until crust is golden brown on the edges. Remove from oven, and serve hot. Enjoy!

GREEN BEAN ORZO WITH TOMATO PESTO

SERVES

··· « 6 ⌣ 8 » ···

This dish is romantically sophisticated but uses simple ingredients and technique. Roasted tomatoes are one of my favorite foods! Among the tomato family, cherry tomatoes are the perfect balance of acid and sweet. When roasted, the acid slightly breaks down, and the sweetness is accentuated and sharpened with bits of charred caramelization. Pesto is a fabulous way to dress up your pastas and vegetables, and you can use less oil if you focus more on other ingredients that contain fats in their natural state, like the raw cashews or walnuts. Doing this doesn't compromise flavor and adds a desirable texture to your finished product.

INGREDIENTS

Orzo
1 lb dried orzo
7–8 C water
1 Tbsp salt

Tomato pesto
3 C cherry tomatoes
½ C raw cashews or walnuts,
   not soaked
2 Tbsp olive oil
3 cloves garlic
1 ½ tsp salt
¼ tsp black pepper

Green beans
12 oz green beans
1 tsp vegetable oil
A few dashes of salt

DIRECTIONS

1. For the orzo, add salt to water and bring to a boil. Add the orzo, and once it boils again, set to a simmer for 15–20 minutes, or until orzo is cooked through. Drain orzo in a colander and run cold water through it. Lightly oil, then set aside.

2. For the tomato pesto, lightly oil tomatoes and dust them with some salt and black pepper. Pop them in the oven at 350 degrees for about 10–15 minutes. Then set to broil for 5 minutes. Take about half the roasted tomatoes and place in a food processor with the cashews or walnuts, olive oil, garlic, salt, and black pepper. Pulse until well incorporated, but slightly grainy.

3. In a large skillet on medium heat, toss the green beans with oil and salt until partly cooked (about 5–7 minutes). Then add the tomato pesto, and mix until beans are well coated, and the pesto is slightly reduced (another 5 minutes or so).

4. Turn off heat. Toss sauce with orzo. Then top with the remaining half of the roasted tomatoes. Enjoy!

ROASTED CARROTS ON LENTILS & FARRO WITH CASHEW SAUCE

SERVES
···« 4 »···

This dish is one of my favorite winter meals and is loaded with rustic, vibrant, and multi-layered flavors. Roasted carrots are such aesthetically beautiful foods. Roasted carrots are partly sweet and pair wonderfully with earthy-flavored grains and legumes, such as farro and lentils. Farro is a fabulous grain that is high in fiber and B vitamins and is a great source of protein, antioxidants, iron, magnesium, and zinc. Pulling this dish together is a fantastic cashew sauce, flavorful yet not overpowering. Plant-based, vegan, yet still incredibly rich and delicious, this dish is sure to impress!

INGREDIENTS

Farro and lentils
3 C water
2 C vegetable stock
1 C farro
1 C lentils
½ red onion, minced
2 tsp vegetable oil
½ tsp salt
½ tsp cumin
¼ tsp paprika
A few dashes of black pepper

Roasted carrots
1 bunch of six colored carrots
2 tsp vegetable oil
½ tsp garlic powder
¼ tsp salt
A dash of black pepper

Cashew sauce
¾ C raw cashew soaked 1–2 hours
1 C water
2 tsp white wine vinegar
1 ½ tsp salt
1 tsp maple syrup
1 tsp lemon juice
2 cloves garlic
2 tsp fresh dill, chopped, mixed in later

Topping: fresh dill, chopped parsley, pomegranate seeds

DIRECTIONS

1. For the farro and lentils, in a medium-sized pot begin by adding in the oil. Once hot, add the onions and sauté until translucent. Add the water and vegetable stock right after. Rinse the lentils and farro using a colander. Place lentils and farro in the pot, and once it boils, set to a simmer for 35–40 minutes. Once done, discard excess water and set aside with lid off to cool.

2. While the farro and lentils are cooking, clean your carrots (no need to peel them). Marinate with garlic powder, oil, salt, and black pepper. Line a small pan with foil or parchment paper. Then roast carrots in an oven at 350 degrees for about 35–40 minutes, or until softened.

3. For the cashew sauce, strain your cashews. Throw all ingredients into a Vitamix or high-speed blender, and blend until perfectly smooth.

4. Place lentils in a dish. Line the carrots. Then top with cashew sauce, pomegranate seeds, fresh dill, and parsley. Enjoy!

REAL-DEAL VEGGIE MEATBALLS

MAKES

···« 25–30 Golf Ball–Sized Meatballs »···

These plant-based meatballs are so delicious and can be paired with spaghetti and marinara or with an array of roasted vegetables. These are made of nearly equal parts of brown rice, mushrooms, walnuts, onions, and crushed pretzels. Brown rice does wonders in producing the holding capacity needed to create meaty textures without the use of eggs! It's also high in fiber as well as B vitamins and minerals. These meatballs count as a complete food since it contains all the macronutrients, with the healthy fat coming from the walnuts, the carbohydrates coming from the brown rice, and the protein coming from the walnuts, rice, and mushrooms! The best part about these meatballs is that they are made with real food, not just the extracted and texturized proteins you find in meat-substitute products.

INGREDIENTS

Meatballs

1 pack of baby portabella mushrooms, chopped
2 C brown rice (measured before cooking)
1 large red onion, chopped
½ of an 8 oz bag of pretzels
¼ C soy sauce
3 Tbsp vegetable oil
2 Tbsp nutritional yeast
2 Tbsp brown sugar
1 tsp black pepper
1 tsp of garlic salt
¼ tsp cayenne pepper

Grilled vegetables

1 pack of colored carrots
1 bunch of asparagus
1 large red onion
1 acorn squash, sliced into rings
1 Tbsp vegetable oil
1 Tbsp of nutritional yeast
1 stalk of fresh rosemary, minced
½ tsp of sea salt
¼ tsp of black pepper

DIRECTIONS

1. For the meatballs, dice the mushrooms and onion and set aside. Follow instructions on your rice packet, and once cooked, set aside to cool.

2. Pulse your pretzels in a food processor until grainy and powdered.

3. Take the rice and place in the food processor until starchy consistency develops.

4. In a large bowl, begin incorporating these ingredients together using your hands, adding oil and spices as you go along.

5. Once completed, line a baking tray with parchment paper and form golf ball–sized servings using your hands to round and compress. Place on the sheet and bake for 35–40 minutes at 350 degrees. Set aside to cool.

6. For the vegetables, cut the veggies and slice your acorn squash into rings. Throw in spices and seasonings. Toss in a bowl. Line another baking tray with parchment paper, and spread veggies evenly. Bake at 350 degrees for 30 minutes, then broil for about 10 minutes. Once baked through, style as desired, recommend as pictured. Enjoy!

COLLARD GREEN RAINBOW WRAPS

MAKES
···« 6 Wraps (12 Halves) »···

I don't think I've ever had so much color in one photo! I absolutely love collard greens because they are such a versatile vegetable. It is one of the best vitamin C–containing foods, and they are a great source of vitamin K and soluble fiber. They also contain multiple potent anticancer fighting properties, such as diindolylmethane and sulforaphane. Loading these beautiful leaves with an array of colorful vegetables and dipping it in a non-oil containing dressing that is laden with layers of flavor, one might say you are actually biting into a rainbow!

INGREDIENTS

Veggies
1 bunch of collard greens (6 leaves)
¼ a red cabbage, thinly sliced
1 C alfalfa sprouts
1 C shredded carrots
1 C sliced cucumber

Crispy tofu
1 pack firm tofu
1 Tbsp vegetable oil
1 Tbsp soy sauce
1 tsp honey

Ginger dressing
½ C cashews, soaked 1–2 hours
¾ C water
1 ½ Tbsp peanut butter
1 Tbsp fresh ginger
1 Tbsp rice vinegar
1 Tbsp lime juice
2 tsp honey
2 garlic cloves
½ tsp turmeric
1 tsp salt
¼ tsp black pepper

Optional: Add a layer of previously cooked brown rice

DIRECTIONS

1. Clean collard green leaves, slice out the center white stem, leaving about 2–3 inches connected at the top of the leaf.

2. Steam collard green leaves individually for no more than 30 seconds each. Set on a flat plate.

3. For the tofu, strain out the fluid, slice into thin slices along the shorter end of the block. Marinate slices with the soy sauce, honey, and oil. Place in a non-stick pan, and fry on medium-high heat until golden brown and caramelization forms. Repeat with the other side. Set strips aside.

4. Set your collard green leaves on a cutting board, place one side of the leaf ¼ of the way on the adjacent side to fill the gap made from cutting out the stem. Layer your ingredients starting with the tofu strip, rice, cabbage, carrots, cucumber and sprouts. Roll the same way you would roll a burrito. Slice right down the middle.

5. For the dressing, put contents into a Vitamix or high-speed blender and blend until perfectly smooth and creamy. Use this as your dipping sauce. Enjoy!

ZUCCHINI CASHEW
RAMEN NOODLES

SERVES
···《 2 》···

If you ask me how I feel about ramen, my response might be something like this: "Ramen is my favorite food, like ever." My tone would be unapologetic, slightly serious, and partly obsessive. Now, take everything you love about ramen and make it just as healthy and nutrient-dense as a salad, and you've created a whole new level of comfort food that feeds your body without leaving your soul out! When I made the dish in the photo, I left nothing for my husband, nothing. And just so you know, zucchinis are loaded with potassium, B vitamins, antioxidants, and fiber. You're welcome.

INGREDIENTS

2 medium-sized zucchinis
2 C broccoli florets
½ red onion, thinly sliced
2 C vegetable broth
¼ C cashews, raw or roasted
¼ C soy sauce
1 Tbsp vegetable or canola oil
2 tsp brown sugar
2 cloves garlic, minced
1 tsp ginger, minced
1 tsp sriracha

Garnish:
Toasted sesame seeds

DIRECTIONS

1. In a small bowl, mix the soy sauce, sugar, and sriracha. Set aside.

2. Using a spiralizer, create your zucchini noodles.

3. Place oil in a pan on medium-high heat. Sauté onion for 2 minutes, and then add the garlic and ginger. Mix for about 30 seconds, then add soy sauce mixture, followed by broccoli and cashews. Once all coated, add the vegetable broth. Add the zucchinis and mix for 2 minutes, or until it is all coated. Remove from heat.

4. Top with toasted sesame seeds and serve immediately. Enjoy!

THAI CURRY VEGGIES & NOODLES

SERVES
··· « 4 ⌣ 6 » ···

People who know me well know I'm pretty obsessed with noodles. Normally, one might have their Thai curry with rice, but why not have it with rice noodles? The components I'm usually looking for in an Asian bowl include everything in this dish, from the slippery noodles, tasty sauce, and lots of veggies. What really brings a Thai curry together is the paste! Make sure you use one that is made using real ingredients, not artificial flavorings. A good curry paste carries the most important flavor elements for this dish, such as the lemongrass, garlic, and chili.

INGREDIENTS

Thai curry sauce
1 can coconut cream
¼ C vegetable broth
3 tsp red curry paste
2 Tbsp lemon
1 Tbsp soy sauce
1 tsp grated ginger
3 cloves garlic, minced
2 tsp brown sugar
½ tsp salt
¼ tsp black pepper
4–5 fresh basil leaves

Tofu
1 pack firm tofu, cut into ½-inch cubes
1 Tbsp vegetable or canola oil
1 Tbsp soy sauce

Veggies
1 red onion, sliced
1 C carrots, julienned
1 C snow peas, whole
1 green bell pepper, sliced
1 poblano pepper, sliced
1 Tbsp vegetable or canola oil

Noodles
1 pack rice noodles, follow instructions on packet
Note: If preferred, serve with basmati rice

Topping: crushed peanuts, sesame seeds, and lemon zest

DIRECTIONS

1. Sauté tofu in a skillet with oil and soy sauce until golden brown edges form. Set aside. Or you can place on a tray with parchment paper and bake in the oven at 375 for 15–20 minutes.

2. Throw ingredients for Thai curry sauce into a food processor until well incorporated.

3. Oil a large pan and toss veggies on high heat for about 2 minutes. Add curry sauce and mix for about 5 minutes, until edges bubble in the pan. Add tofu cubes and mix until coated.

4. For the rice noodles, follow the directions on the packet. Once ready, run under cold water to stop the cooking process. Strain. Add rice noodles to veggies and curry and lightly mix. Top with sesame seeds, lemon zest, and crushed peanuts. Enjoy!

ORANGE TOFU BOWL

SERVES
··· « 3 ∽ 4 » ···

This is a fun spin on the popular Asian orange chicken, but here I added loads of broccoli and used tofu instead! This is such a tasty way to transform your ordinary orange juice into a savory masterpiece. You'll find that this dish works fantastic for either a dinner party or a meal prep option. From the pleasing sweetness to hints of garlic, ginger, and beautifully layered flavors, you might forget this sauce is made mostly of freshly squeezed orange juice. Every bite is perfectly coated with just the right amount of tangy yumminess!

INGREDIENTS

Tofu and veggies

1 pack extra-firm tofu, cut in cubes
1 16 oz bag broccoli florets
2 shallots, diced
1 Tbsp cornstarch
3 cloves garlic, minced
1 Tbsp ginger, minced
1 Tbsp vegetable oil
1 tsp soy sauce

Orange sauce

1½ C orange juice + 2 Tbsp water
3 Tbsp cornstarch
1 Tbsp coconut sugar, or
    brown sugar
2 Tbsp soy sauce
2 tsp sriracha
1 tsp sesame oil

Jasmine rice

1 ½ C jasmine rice, rinsed
2 ¾ C water
¼ tsp salt

Topping

2–3 Tbsp green onion, chopped
1 tsp sesame seeds

DIRECTIONS

1. For the rice, either follow the instructions on your packet or the following: Place water in a medium-sized pot on high heat. Add salt. Once boiling, add the rice. Then set to simmer for 15 minutes. Turn off heat and lightly turn the over rice. Then cover with the lid.

2. For the orange tofu, begin by adding 1 Tbsp of starch to your tofu and drizzle a little soy sauce. Lightly toss to coat the tofu. In a large skillet on medium-high heat, place 1 Tbsp of vegetable oil. Add the shallots and stir for a minute or so. Then add the tofu and cook until all sides are crispy and golden brown. Now add the garlic and ginger and sauté for 1–2 minutes. Then add the broccoli and toss for another 2 minutes. Turn off heat.

3. In a saucepan, add the orange juice and remaining 3 Tbsp of cornstarch, along with the soy sauce, sugar, sriracha, and sesame oil. Use a whisk and mix until thickened. If too thick, add a little of the water. Once thickened, add to the tofu and veggies pan. Mix on medium heat for about 2–3 minutes, until all coated and incorporated. Serve over rice and top with green onion and sesame seeds. Enjoy!

TEMPEH & KALE BUDDHA BOWL

SERVES

···≪ 4 ≫···

If you're looking for a clean, protein-dense, and easy meal prep option to get you through the week, then this is it! Since I find that tempeh can be a little strong, I like to add tofu to help balance out some of the overpowering flavors. Lacinato kale is so rich with nutrients and is one of the hardiest greens you can come across. Few of us realize the potential of simply baking a sweet potato, but there are so many sweet and flowery flavors that we lose when we do too much to them. This dish appreciates and maintains the simplicity of the humble sweet potato, while still giving you everything you want in a classic Buddha bowl!

INGREDIENTS

Yams, baked whole, sliced

Tempeh & kale

8 oz tempeh, cubed
½ pack firm tofu, cubed
3 C lacinato kale
1 can black beans
½ medium red onion, chopped
¼ C vegetable broth
2 Tbsp soy sauce
1 Tbsp vegetable or canola oil
1 Tbsp maple syrup
1 tsp sesame oil
1 tsp ginger, minced
½ tsp salt
¼ tsp black pepper

Quinoa

1 C tricolor quinoa
1 C vegetable broth
1 C water
¼ tsp salt

Garnish:

Black sesame seeds

DIRECTIONS

1. Sauté onions with vegetable oil for about 3 minutes on high heat, until clear. Add your tofu and tempeh, and cook until edges are browned. Once browned, add the soy sauce and reduce to medium heat. Add remaining ingredients and seasonings, saving the kale for the last step. Add kale and toss for about 2 minutes, just to barely wilt them.

2. For the quinoa, rinse thoroughly and strain. Set water and broth in a medium-sized pot on high heat. Add quinoa and salt. Once boiling, set to a simmer for 15–20 minutes. Stir quinoa, then let cool for a few minutes.

3. For the yams, bake at 400 degrees for 35–40 minutes, until cooked through.

4. Serve Buddha bowl as shown or preferred, sprinkle black sesame seeds. Enjoy!

CHICKPEA MASALA

SERVES

··· « 4 ⁓ 6 » ···

This flavorful multilayered Indian-style chickpea masala is one of my husband's favorite dishes! I usually make it for him as a meal prep option. You can pick up a ready-made garam masala spice mix from most higher-end food markets. It includes cinnamon, cloves, cumin, black pepper, and my two favorites, cardamom and coriander. Cardamom and coriander have similar health benefits. They can be used to naturally treat high blood pressure, high blood sugar, and digestive issues. The best part is that they both have a subtle floral flavor that gives such a complementary twist to this onion- and garlic-infused dish.

INGREDIENTS

2 cans garbanzo beans
1 can coconut cream
2 cans fire-roasted tomatoes
1 large white onion, chopped
2 Tbsp vegetable oil
1 Tbsp ginger, minced
3 cloves of garlic, minced
2 ½ tsp garam masala
1 tsp salt
Juice of half a lime
A few dashes of cayenne pepper

Basmati rice
1 ½ C rice (follow instructions)

Topping
Fresh cilantro, chopped

DIRECTIONS

1. Place oil in a medium-sized pot on high heat. Once hot, add the chopped onion and sauté. Once softened and golden (about 5–7 minutes), add garlic and ginger. Mix for 1–2 minutes.

2. Add the fire-roasted tomatoes.

3. Add the coconut cream.

4. Strain the garbanzo beans, rinse under water, and add to the pot.

5. After mixing, set to medium heat for about 5–7 minutes.

6. Add the garam masala, salt, lime juice, and cayenne pepper. Mix well, and set to simmer for about 10–15 minutes, until flavors have well dispersed throughout the pot.

7. In the meantime, prepare your rice. Follow the instructions on your pack.

8. Once ready, turn off heat for both the rice and chickpea masala. Place rice in a bowl and top with a generous portion of the chickpea masala, with a garnish of fresh cilantro. Enjoy!

CHIPOTLE-STYLE BEANS & RICE

SERVES
··· « 3 ⁓ 4 » ···

Truth be told, one of the healthiest "fast food" selections right now has to be Chipotle, based on the options you choose of course! It's become one of my favorite go-to restaurants when I'm on the run but still want something satisfying and nutritious. I usually go for either the salad or bowl and pack it with brown rice, black beans, veggies, and extra lettuce! Most of the time I'll skip out on the sour cream and cheese and focus on a hefty helping of guacamole and the yummy salsas! This recipe is a simple spin on my favorite combination for the Chipotle bowl!

INGREDIENTS

Rice
1 C brown basmati rice
2 C water
½ C vegetable broth
½ C cilantro, chopped
¼ tsp salt

Black beans
3 cans black beans
½ red onion, chopped
1 chipotle, in adobo sauce, minced
1 Tbsp lime juice
2 tsp vegetable oil
½ tsp salt

Salsa
2 tomatoes, chopped
½ red onion, chopped
⅓ C cilantro, chopped
1 Tbsp lime juice
¼ tsp salt

Lettuce
2 heads romaine lettuce,
   sliced finely

Guacamole
See Guacamole recipe on
   page 173

DIRECTIONS

1. For rice, place water, vegetable broth, and salt in a pot with basmati rice. Bring to a boil, then let simmer for 15–20 minutes, until all fluid is absorbed. Once cooked through, remove lid, fluff rice, leave lid off. Once partly cooled, add chopped cilantro and lime juice. Mix.

2. For the beans, pour oil and sauté the red onion in a medium-sized skillet on high heat for about 2–3 minutes. Add the black beans, chopped chipotle, juice, salt, and remaining ingredients. Mix for about 3–5 minutes. Turn off heat. Set aside.

3. For the salsa, mix the ingredients in a small bowl.

4. For guacamole, see guacamole recipe on page 165.

5. Serve with rice on the base, and top with beans, lettuce, salsa, and guacamole. Enjoy!

HATCH CHILI JACKFRUIT TACOS

MAKES
··· « 10 ～ 12 Tacos » ···

The Hatch chili is native to New Mexico and is best prepared by charring over an open flame. It is rich in vitamins A and C, and also dietary fiber. Hatch chilies contain capsaicin, which is a substance that occurs naturally in chili peppers and lends itself to the degree of spiciness. Capsaicin contains anti-inflammatory properties, which is why it's been found, in some cases, to minimize pain. When it comes to jackfruit, think beauty food! It can help to limit the appearance of wrinkles and promotes healthy hair and skin. It also is high in protein and can help prevent indigestion. With just the right seasonings and trimmings, you can have yourself one lean, mean, plant-based taco!

INGREDIENTS

Jackfruit
2 cans jackfruit
½ can fire-roasted tomatoes,
   drained (optional)
1 ½ Tbsp vegetable oil
½ white onion, brunoised
2 ½ Tbsp taco seasoning
2 Tbsp ketchup
1 tsp honey
½ tsp paprika
½ tsp salt
¼ tsp black pepper
¼ tsp cumin

Hatch chilies
Fire-roasted, dash of salt,
   seeds removed

Toppings
½ white cabbage, julienned
½ purple cabbage, julienned
2 barely ripe mangos, brunoised
½ white onion, brunoised
½ red onion, brunoised
½ C radishes, sliced
½ C cilantro, minced
Juice of 2 limes

White sauce
½ C vegan mayonnaise
Juice of 1 lime
½ tsp onion powder
1 tsp salt
¼ tsp black pepper

Flour or corn taco tortillas

DIRECTIONS

1. Prep all your vegetables (add a little lime juice to each prep).

2. Strain jackfruit. Place in a pot with water to cover contents. Set to high heat. Let boil for about 2 minutes. Turn off heat, strain, and wash with cool water. Once cooled, pull apart. Set aside.

3. If you prefer a wetter jackfruit filling, add the fire-roasted tomatoes. If you prefer a dryer, meatier feel, do not add it. Place oil in a pan. Set to high heat. Sauté onions for 1–2 minutes. Add the jackfruit, toss for 1–2 minutes. Add the taco seasoning and toss. Once well coated, add the ketchup and remaining seasonings. Cook for about 5 minutes. Turn off heat and let cool.

4. Place tortillas on a pan in the oven at 350 degrees on broil for 5 minutes.

5. For your Hatch chilies, remove stem, slice in half across, and scrape out seeds (will be very spicy if you don't).

6. For the white sauce, place all ingredients in a bowl and mix until well incorporated. Transfer to a squeeze bottle to drizzle.

7. Build your tacos! Style as desired. Recommendation: Start with jackfruit, slice of Hatch chili, top with cabbage, onion, mango, radish, white sauce, cilantro, and squeeze of lime. Enjoy!

VEGGIE QUESADILLAS

Quesadillas are one of my favorite foods to have in Mexican cuisine! Normally, you'd think of a quesadilla as something that is calorically dense, high in saturated fat, and obviously not dairy free because of cheese. I created my own cheese from scratch using cashew sauce and tapioca, making this quesadilla saturated fat-free! Pairing this delicious filling with nutritious homemade tortillas makes this a winning meal!

INGREDIENTS

8 Tortillas

See page 177 for homemade
    tortilla recipe

Cheese

½ C raw cashews, soaked
    1–2 hours
2 C water
3 ½ Tbsp tapioca flour
2 Tbsp nutritional yeast
1 Tbsp lime juice
1 tsp onion powder
1 tsp garlic powder
1 ½ tsp salt
½ tsp brown sugar
A few dashes of black pepper

Veggies

1 can black beans, strained
    and rinsed
1 can sweet corn, strained
    and rinsed
2 red bell peppers, brunoised
¼ C sliced pickled jalapeños
½ bunch fresh cilantro
1 Tbsp lime juice

DIRECTIONS

1. For the "cheese," throw all the ingredients into a Vitamix or high-speed blender. Blend until perfectly smooth. Pour into a small pot and continuously stir using a spatula on medium-high heat until boiling. Then set heat to low, and you will notice it will begin to get thick and sticky, like melted cheese. When you can, scrape the bottom of your pot clean with your spatula. If the cheese slowly folds back in, it should be ready. Remove from heat, cover, and set aside.

2. For the veggies, toss in a bowl with lime juice.

3. To build your quesadilla, place one tortilla on your heated pan. Add a few spoons of your veggie-bean mix and some more sliced jalapeños (optional), then drizzle a generous amount of your melted cheese. Place another tortilla on top, and press. Heat for a minute until warmed through, remove, and slice. Enjoy!

Soups

Stews

SLOW COOKER
SWEET POTATO CHILI STEW

SERVES UP TO

···≪ 8 ≫···

Using a slow cooker is one of the best ways to tenderize and accentuate the flavors of your food, while sneaking in a wide variety of veggies! Sweet potatoes are loaded with vitamin A, which is important for the skin and eyesight. Adding quinoa adds complex carbs that have a long-acting effect on blood sugar and keeps you feeling fuller longer. Also, the quinoa combined with the black beans produces complete amino acids! This healthy, hardy meal is sure to become a family favorite!

Great option for meal prep

INGREDIENTS

3 C sweet potato, cubed

1 large red onion, chopped

1 red bell pepper, chopped

1 green bell pepper, chopped

3 cans black beans

1 can fire-roasted tomatoes

¾ C quinoa

1 carton vegetable broth

4 cloves of garlic, minced

1 Tbsp oil

2 ½ tsp cumin

2 tsp paprika

1 ½ tsp chili powder

1 ½ tsp salt (add more as desired)

¼ tsp black pepper

Topping

Avocado slices

Red chili flakes

Cilantro

DIRECTIONS

1. Prep veggies.

2. Pour vegetable broth into slow cooker pot. Set at high for about 4 hours. (It may be ready before then. Check at 3 hours and 30 minutes.) After the first 20 minutes, add all the remaining ingredients, and mix. Cover with lid, and check every hour to give it a light mix.

3. Once ready, remove lid, and let it cool for a few minutes. Plate it, and top with chili flakes, avocado, and cilantro. Enjoy!

BALILA

SERVES

··· « 2 ⁓ 3 » ···

Balila is a traditional dish, native to my home country of Lebanon in the Middle East. The Lebanese like to have it for breakfast with freshly baked pita bread, or as one of the many options of a traditional meza spread for an evening dinner. It's so easy to make, yet full of flavor, and it's loaded with nutrients, especially protein, since it's predominantly chickpeas. The garlic and cumin are the leading flavors that are balanced beautifully with the sourness of lemon, followed by the lingering smoothness of extra virgin olive oil, and topped with perfectly toasted pine nuts. Scrumptiously delicious!

INGREDIENTS

2 can garbanzo beans, drained
2 C water
Juice of half a lemon
3 cloves of garlic, mashed
2 tsp of cumin
1 Tbsp olive oil
½ tsp salt
A few dashes of black pepper
A few dashes of cayenne pepper

Topping
Toasted pine nuts
¼ C chopped parsley

Bread
Lavash or pita bread

DIRECTIONS

1. Toast pine nuts in a pan until lightly browned. Set aside.

2. Place garbanzo beans in a small pot with the water. Set aside about ¼ C of whole garbanzos to garnish with. Cook for about 5–7 minutes on medium heat.

3. Add lemon juice, olive oil, cumin, salt, and black pepper.

4. With a large fork, mash some of the beans to create more layers on the plate. Then add the whole garbanzos.

5. After cooking, add the mashed garlic.

6. While plating, add a few more dashes of cumin, cayenne pepper, and top with fresh parsley and the toasted pine nuts. Enjoy!

KIBBE
WITH CARROT & SQUASH SOUP

SERVES
···« 8 ～ 10 »···

Ok, so I'll admit a bit of work goes into creating this masterpiece, but you don't have to be a professional chef to make it! To give you some background behind this dish, my father is Lebanese, but my mother is part Egyptian and part Iraqi. This dish is native to Iraq. It has earthy and sophisticated flavors from the onion-infused, textured protein packed into a perfectly cooked bulgur pocket to the rich carrot and squash soup that is just as savory as it is sweet. This dish is a treasure in a bowl! I always feel especially loved when Mom prepares this for the family!

KIBBE INGREDIENTS

Kibbe (outer layer)
2 C of fine bulgur
2 ½ C water (add more if needed)
2 C semolina
A few dashes of cinnamon
1 tsp salt

Kibbe stuffing
1 C textured soy protein
3 medium onions, finely chopped
½ C walnuts, chopped
2 Tbsp flour
1 tsp allspice
1 tsp salt
¼ tsp black pepper
¼ tsp nutmeg

Boiling broth for kibbe
4 quarts water
1 tsp cinnamon
1 bay leaf
1 tsp salt
⅓ tsp allspice
¼ a seed of cardamom
½ tsp black pepper

KIBBE DIRECTIONS

1. Soak the bulgur in water. (You're going to add enough water until you have a formable dough, this may be more or less than 2 ½ C.) Mix together with semolina with a dash of cinnamon and 1 tsp salt. Knead until sticky. Divide into 24 balls.

2. Mix the textured soy protein and walnuts with the rest of the spices to create the stuffing.

3. Make a deep pocket in each ball of bulgur/semolina mix and place a heaping Tbsp of the stuffing into the pocket. Close together to form a round, flattened patty.

4. Bring the broth with its mixed ingredients to a boil. Drop the patties one by one into the boiling broth and cook for 45 minutes. Remove each patty out of the broth and allow to cool on a cooling rack.

SOUP INGREDIENTS & DIRECTIONS >>

KIBBE WITH CARROT & SQUASH SOUP (CONT.)

You're almost there! The most difficult part is behind you. This savory squash soup is simple and rich in flavor and absolutely perfect when paired with the kibbe on the previous page.

SOUP INGREDIENTS

3 quarts water
12–15 carrots, cut into chunks
1 white onion, cut into chunks
2 cups squash, 1-inch cubes
1 Tbsp brown sugar
1 tsp cinnamon
1 tsp salt
¼ tsp black pepper
2 pieces of crushed cardamom
1 tsp garlic salt
Dash of dried mint
1 bay leaf
1 tsp ginger, grated
Juice from half a medium lemon
½ C celery, chopped

SOUP DIRECTIONS

1. Place carrots and onion in boiling water until soft. Then puree in a Vitamix or high-speed blender using water you cooked it with. Pour back into your cooking pot and add the chopped celery. Precook squash separately and add to the soup. Add all spices. Bring to another boil. Turn off heat.

2. Place kibbe patty or two in a bowl and pour carrot squash soup on top. Enjoy!

BROCCOLI SOUP

SERVES

···« 3 ⌣ 4 »···

There's nothing like a warm bowl of broccoli soup on a cold winter's day. This is one of my favorite go-to comfort foods when I have a lot of broccoli I need to use up! And broccoli just so happens to be one my favorite vegetables, so it works out perfectly! Loaded with protein and essential vitamins and nutrients, broccoli does a great job filling you up without the unwanted calories. This recipe is so luxuriously rich and creamy, I promise you it will be hard to have just one serving! This is a simple classic made effortlessly nutritious and delicious!

INGREDIENTS

16 oz fresh broccoli florets

2 ¼ C vegetable broth

2 C water

1 C raw cashew, soaked for 2 hours

½ medium onion, finely diced

3 cloves of garlic

3 Tbsp nutritional yeast

1 Tbsp flour

1 Tbsp vegetable oil

1 ½ tsp salt

¼ tsp black pepper

A few dashes of cayenne

DIRECTIONS

1. Place the soaked cashews and garlic with 1 C of water in a Vitamix or high-speed blender, and blend until completely smooth and creamy. Add the second cup of water and run again. Once well mixed, add the vegetable broth, flour, nutritional yeast, salt, black pepper, and cayenne, and give it one more blend. This is the cream base for your soup.

2. In a medium-sized pot, pour the oil and set to medium-high heat. Sauté the onion until transparent. Add the cream base, and continue to mix lightly for a few minutes.

3. Once it boils, add about ¼ of the broccoli (loosely chopped into smaller pieces). Then add the remaining whole broccoli florets. Set to a simmer with the lid on for about 7–10 minutes, depending on how well-done you like your broccoli to be. I prefer it slightly undercooked, as I like the texture of stiffer broccoli.

4. Serve with whole wheat artisan bread. Enjoy!

VEGGIE LENTIL SOUP

SERVES

··« 6 ⁓ 8 »··

If you're looking for a perfectly charming lentil stew, then look no further! When my husband and I first got married, this was one of his favorite meal prep dishes. It did the job of filling him up, while making him feel like he wasn't missing out on anything because it tasted so good! It also holds really well in the fridge and just needs to be microwaved when ready to eat. This stew is packed full of protein and a handsome helping of vegetables in every serving. There are days I can't wait for lunchtime or dinner just to have it!

INGREDIENTS

16 oz bag lentils

2 C celery, chopped

2 C carrots, chopped

1 C yams or regular potato, cubed

1 large red onion, chopped

1 carton vegetable stock

1 can fire-roasted tomato chunks

Juice of half a lemon

1 ½ tsp ginger, minced

3–4 cloves of garlic, minced

2–3 tsp salt, add more or less
  as desired

1 Tbsp vegetable oil

1 ½ tsp cumin

¼ tsp of black pepper

¼ tsp celery spice

¼ tsp dried rosemary

A few dashes of cayenne pepper

Topping
Fresh parsley

DIRECTIONS

1. Sauté onions for 2–3 minutes on medium-high heat with the vegetable oil. Then add ginger and garlic, and stir for a minute or two. Then add the carrots, and stir. Then add the celery.

2. Once cooked down for about 2 minutes, add the lentils. Stir again until all the lentils are coated. Then add a full carton of vegetable stock and leave to boil. Once boiling, add 4–5 C of water. Add the yams (or regular potato) and fire-roasted tomato chunks, and let simmer for 20–25 minutes.

3. Add the spices and seasonings, and let simmer again for 10–15 minutes.

4. Check lentils. If soft, turn off heat. If a little hard, continue to simmer for another 10 minutes. Overall cooking time should be between 30–40 minutes.

5. Garnish with fresh parsley. Enjoy!

TURKISH LENTIL SOUP

SERVES

···« 8 ‒ 10 »···

This is a traditional Turkish red lentil soup. This perfectly savory soup is so easy to make, you'll love it from the first time you try it. Red lentils are a powerhouse of nutrients, protein, and fiber and are a wonderful source of folate and magnesium. I personally like this soup to be on the salty side, and the more cumin the better! So bear in mind the ingredients here are merely suggestions. Feel free to add more of whatever you feel your taste buds are craving!

INGREDIENTS

1 large yellow onion, chopped
1 garlic clove, minced
4 C water
4 C vegetable broth
1 ½ C red lentils
1 Tbsp vegetable oil
1 ¼ tsp salt
1 ½ tsp cumin
½ tsp turmeric
¼ tsp black pepper
¼ tsp cayenne pepper

Topping
A drizzle of olive oil
Fresh thyme

DIRECTIONS

1. Begin by sautéing onion in oil for about 3–4 minutes. Add garlic, then add broth and water, followed by lentils and seasonings.

2. Bring to a boil, then simmer for 20 minutes.

3. Let cool for a few minutes. Then transfer to a Vitamix or high-speed blender, and blend until smooth.

4. Serve with a drizzle of olive oil and fresh thyme. Enjoy!

CLASSIC TOMATO SOUP

SERVES

···《 3 ᜡ 4 》···

Among all the soups in the world, there's nothing quite like the timeless classic tomato soup. There's also nothing quite like making your own from scratch rather than having it straight out of a can. Tomatoes are high in an antioxidant called lycopene, which carries protective factors, such as lowering the risk of heart disease and even cancer. Tomatoes are also a good source of vitamin C, potassium, folate, and vitamin K. I like my supplements in a bowl where I can smell, taste, and enjoy them! Hope you enjoy this splendidly humble yet traditional classic!

INGREDIENTS

Soup

1 can roasted tomato chunks

1 6 oz can tomato paste

2 C vegetable broth

2 C water

½ white onion, chopped

½ C raw cashews, soaked 1–2 hours

2 tsp olive oil

1 tsp brown sugar

1 ¼ tsp salt

½ tsp dried basil

¼ tsp black pepper

White garlic sauce (optional)

½ C raw cashews, soaked 1–2 hours

⅓ C water

2 Tbsp lemon juice

1 tsp olive oil

1 clove of garlic

½ tsp white wine vinegar

Salt and pepper, to taste

DIRECTIONS

1. Place the cashews, onion, and 1 C of water in a food processor until perfectly smooth and creamy. Add tomato chunks, followed by the tomato paste, and process until smooth. Add vegetable stock and pulse until fully incorporated.

2. Set a pot on medium-high heat. Add your mixture, and begin to stir. Add the last C of water. While stirring, add the remaining ingredients.

3. Bring to a boil, then let simmer for 5–7 minutes.

4. Turn off heat and serve while hot with artisan bread. For the white garlic sauce, throw contents into a high-speed blender or Vitamix, and blend until smooth and creamy. Adjust the recipe for desired consistency. Enjoy!

ARTICHOKE & LEEK STEW

SERVES UP TO

···≪ 8 ≫···

The artichoke has to be one of the most opulent of vegetables, with its beautiful build, soft meaty texture of its heart, unique taste, and subtle sweetness. Complimenting the artichoke is the humble leek, audacious in flavor, and unapologetic in nutrients, it is a very good source of folate, iron, B6, and vitamins A, C, and K. You might have noticed by now that the base of several of these vegetable stews and soups is cashews, which is such a blessing to the plant-based community in creating the creamy consistency we love in our soups!

INGREDIENTS

1 quart of vegetable broth

1 large leek, diced

1 yellow onion, chopped

1 C of raw cashews, soaked
   1–2 hours

2 cans of artichoke hearts,
   or 12 oz frozen

2–3 C fresh spinach

1 can black beans

2 Tbsp of lemon juice

1 Tbsp vegetable oil

1 ¼ tsp sea salt

¼ tsp black pepper

Dash of cayenne pepper

Topping
Chives

Pine nuts

See directions for
   added water content

DIRECTIONS

1. Start by sautéing leek and onion with vegetable oil for about 5 minutes in a large pot. Stir frequently.

2. While the onions and leaks are sautéing, strain the soaked cashews, and throw into a high-speed blender or Vitamix. Add 2 cups of water, and process until completely smooth. Add the vegetable broth to the blender, and pulse until fully incorporated with cashew mix.

3. Add soupy consistency to the sautéing onion and leeks. Mix for a few minutes. Once boiling, turn heat to a simmer. Add artichoke hearts and black beans. Allow to simmer for 10 minutes. Then add the lemon, salt, pepper, and cayenne.

4. After mixing in the seasonings, add the fresh spinach and cook down until wilted, about 2–3 minutes. Then turn off the heat.

5. Serve into bowls while hot. Garnish with chives and pine nuts. Enjoy!

Sal

nds

ROASTED VEGGIE & KALE SALAD WITH TURMERIC DRESSING

SERVES
···« 4 ⁓ 6 »···

This is my husband's number one favorite salad! Crisp Tuscan kale topped with roasted veggies, a creamy turmeric dressing, and little bursts of pomegranate seeds, everything you're looking for in a salad to satisfy your taste buds and your hunger! The dressing is fantastic and holds well in a mason jar in the fridge for up to a week! There's so many vitamins, minerals, and antioxidants in every bite. Turmeric contains anti-inflammatory properties, so combined with all the other nutrient-dense foods here, you can definitely say this dish is medicine on a plate.

INGREDIENTS

10 oz Tuscan kale
16 oz true Belgian brussels sprouts
2 medium-sized yams
2 C broccoli florets
1 ½ Tbsp vegetable oil
1 tsp salt
1 tsp ground rosemary
¼ tsp black pepper

Turmeric dressing

¾ C cashews, soaked 1–2 hours
1 C water
1 Tbsp white wine vinegar
2 tsp maple syrup
A squeeze of lemon
2 cloves of garlic
1 tsp salt
½ tsp turmeric
¼ tsp black pepper

Topping

½ C pomegranate seeds
2 Tbsp toasted pumpkin seeds
2 Tbsp toasted pistachio

DIRECTIONS

1. Chop kale lightly. Set aside as the base.

2. Cut yams into ½-inch squares.

3. In a large pan, toss brussels sprouts, yams, and broccoli with oil, salt, rosemary, and pepper. Place in the oven on bake for about 25–30 minutes at 375 degrees, or until cooked through. Then set to broil for 5 minutes. Once slightly cooled, scoop on the Tuscan kale.

4. For the dressing, throw all contents into a Vitamix or high-speed blender, and blend until perfectly smooth and creamy. You can store the extra dressing in a Mason jar in the fridge for up to a week.

5. Top with a generous portion of pomegranate seeds and the toasted pistachios and pumpkin seeds. Then drizzle the turmeric dressing. Enjoy!

SWEET POTATO NOODLES WITH RED PEPPER GINGER DRESSING

SERVES
···« 2 ⁓ 3 »···

It's one thing to eat your salad with a fork, it's a whole other thing to eat it with chopsticks! I can tell you my husband was a little confused but quite delighted when I first presented him with this dish! This is my snoodle salad, a play on sweet potatoes in noodle form! Sweet potatoes are high in the antioxidant beta-carotene and are a wonderful starchy veggie to incorporate in your daily diet since it helps to keep you full longer, while still being a rich source of fiber. The fire-roasted red pepper sauce is the perfect balance of sweet, tangy, and spicy!

INGREDIENTS

Sweet potato noodles

1 large (or two medium)
   sweet potatoes
1 ½ Tbsp vegetable oil
1 C purple cabbage, shredded
½ C parsley, chopped
3 Tbsp green onion, chopped

Red pepper ginger dressing

2 fire-roasted red peppers
Juice of one small orange
2 Tbsp olive oil
1 Tbsp lemon juice
1–2 Tbsp water, depending on
   desired thickness
1 Tbsp peanut butter
2 garlic cloves
1 tsp salt
1 tsp white wine vinegar
1 tsp grated ginger
½ tsp maple syrup
¼ tsp black pepper

Topping

Green onion
Toasted sesame seeds

DIRECTIONS

1. Create noodles by running your sweet potato through a spiralizer.

2. Lightly oil a nonstick pan and set to medium-high heat. Sauté sweet potato noodles for 5–10 minutes, or until partly softened. Set aside.

3. Throw all the contents of the dressing into a Vitamix or high-speed blender, and blend until smooth.

4. Add cabbage, parsley, and green onion to the sweet potato noodles. Toss noodles with ¼ C of dressing, or more as desired. Top with toasted sesame seeds and green onion. Enjoy!

THE INCREDIBLE ASIAN SALAD

SERVES
···《 4 》···

If I took all my favorite vegetables and favorite protein source and tastefully put an Asian flare on it, then this would be it! The nutrient profile of this dish is so dense! Whenever you see a rainbow of color with dark green leafy veggies, you know you're about to consume a dynamo of antioxidants and fiber! The textures and flavors of the carrot, radicchio, eggplant, baby broccoli, arugula, and green leaf lettuce marry wonderfully with the perfectly balanced Asian-style dressing, with the beautiful flavors of ginger and garlic coming through. I hope you enjoy this "curling on the couch" worthy super salad!

INGREDIENTS

1 head leaf lettuce
1 pack arugula
1 large carrot, julienned or shredded
1 small head radicchio

Grilled tofu
1 packet pack extra-firm tofu
2 tsp vegetable oil
2 tsp soy sauce
1 tsp honey

Grilled veggies
1 bunch baby broccoli
1 medium-sized eggplant
2 tsp soy sauce
1 tsp vegetable oil

Dressing
2 Tbsp water
1 ½ Tbsp soy sauce
1 Tbsp rice wine vinegar
2 cloves of garlic, minced
2 tsp vegetable oil
1 tsp ginger, minced
1 tsp brown sugar
1 tsp lime juice
½ tsp gomasio

DIRECTIONS

1. Loosely chop leaf lettuce and mix with arugula. Set aside.

2. Slice radicchio into strips. Set aside. Place carrots in a small bowl.

3. For the tofu, slice your block, then cut into triangles. Marinate with your oil, honey, and soy sauce. Place on the grill until cooked through with grill marks.

4. For the eggplant, cut out the inner section, then slice into thick strips. Marinate and sauté until softened. Remove from the pan. After marinating the baby broccoli, lightly cook it using the same pan.

5. For the dressing, whisk all the ingredients in a small bowl.

6. To build the salad, create a base of lettuce and arugula. Top with radicchio, then carrots, and arrange the grilled tofu and veggies to surround the mound. Pour dressing and top with a sprinkle of gomasio. Enjoy!

ROASTED ACORN SQUASH SALAD

SERVES

··· « 3 ⌣ 4 » ···

I love to layer different textures and flavors with my salads. The more the better! Here we have fresh, peppery arugula, bits of quinoa, bursts of sweet goji berries, crispy and caramelized edges of acorn squash enveloping the soft meatiness of the centers, and the toasted pecans, all pulled together with an insatiably savory balsamic vinaigrette reduction. Is your mouth watering? Because mine is! Acorn squash is a powerhouse of vitamins and minerals, containing high amounts of vitamin C, thiamin, potassium, and manganese. The day I made this salad, I had to quickly pack it up and get on the road with my husband (then fiancé), since we were on schedule to pick up our couch, preparing for our first place together. We had to rent a truck; he drove while I fed him. All the while I was thinking, *What a lucky guy this is!* Ha.

INGREDIENTS

Acorn squash
2 medium-sized acorn squash
2 Tbsp vegetable oil
1 Tbsp raw honey
2 tsp cornstarch (to enhance
   crispiness)
½ tsp salt
¼ tsp black pepper
1 medium-sized garlic clove,
   crushed

Quinoa
½ C quinoa
1 C water

Balsamic reduction
¼ C balsamic vinegar
2 tsp raw honey
½ tsp sea salt
1 clove of garlic, mashed (added
   once cooled)
A few dashes of black pepper

Salad
7 oz baby arugula, or as needed
Juice of 1 small lime
2 tsp olive oil

Toppings
Crushed pecans
Vegan cheese crumble, optional
Goji berries

DIRECTIONS

1. For the acorn squash, slice into less than half an inch circles, take out seeded center. Mix oil, honey, seasonings, garlic, and cornstarch, and pour on a plate. Place rings on plate and smother with seasoning, front and back and insides. Set oven to 350 degrees. Place on a nonstick pan and bake for 20 minutes. Then broil at 400 degrees for 5–10 minutes, until caramelization appears.

2. For the quinoa, follow instructions on your pack.

3. Dress the salad with lime and olive oil, then toss with cooled quinoa.

4. For the balsamic reduction, place the ingredients in a tiny pot and set to medium-high heat until boiling. Then set to low heat for 1–2 minutes while mixing. Repeat this process once or twice. Then set aside to cool. Once cooled, add fresh garlic. You should end up with a syrupy, thicker consistency.

5. Top beautifully grilled acorn squash on salad, followed by the crushed pecans, and goji berries. Then drizzle your balsamic reduction. Enjoy!

ARUGULA SALAD WITH BARTLETT PEAR VINAIGRETTE & CANDIED PECANS

SERVES

···《 4 》···

Yes, you can buy ready-made candied pecans, but it's pretty fun to make this healthier version yourself! As you can see, a lot of these salads include arugula, and that's because it is a powerhouse of nutrients. It contains the highest concentration of nitrates in the super greens family. Nitrates can turn into nitric oxide, which helps to dilate blood vessels and lower blood pressure and, in turn, protects against chronic diseases. It also helps to boost athletic performance and increase immunity. The best way I've found to eat my bitter greens is to create beautifully simple vinaigrettes that are plant-based (mostly made out of fruit). Here, I paired it with a Bartlett pear vinaigrette, perfectly sweet, tart, and loaded with flavor!

INGREDIENTS

1 7 oz bag arugula
½ C pomegranate seeds
1–2 Bartlett pears, thinly sliced
2 oz vegan cheese (optional)

Vinaigrette

1 Bartlett pear
1 C water
1 shallot
1 ½ Tbsp olive oil
1 Tbsp white wine vinegar
2 tsp Dijon mustard
1 tsp lemon juice
1 tsp maple syrup
1 ¼ tsp salt
¼ tsp black pepper

Candied pecans

(**Note:** *Make your own or use ready-made candied pecans.*)
1 C pecans
2 Tbsp coconut or brown sugar
1 Tbsp maple syrup
1 tsp vegetable oil
¼ tsp salt
A few dashes of cinnamon

DIRECTIONS

1. For the vinaigrette, remove seeds from pear. Place all ingredients in a Vitamix or high-speed blender, and blend until completely smooth. Set aside.

2. For the candied pecans, mix pecans with ingredients. Line a pan with parchment paper or foil. Place in a toaster oven at 300 degrees for about 7–10 minutes. Then flip them around using a spatula and leave them in for another 7–10 minutes. Remove from the oven and set aside to cool.

3. Place arugula in a bowl and top with pomegranate seeds, slices of pear, vegan cheese (if desired), and the candied pecans. Drizzle Bartlett pear vinaigrette on top. Enjoy!

CAESAR SALAD

SERVES

···《 4 ∽ 6 》···

Who doesn't love a good Caesar salad? Except here we're not using any eggs, cheese, and very little vegan mayonnaise. Some Caesar salad recipes call for one full cup of mayo! Again, here we are harnessing the creaminess of soaked cashews to mimic the rich dressing of the classic Caesar salad. This way you're getting a handsome helping of greens and nutrient-dense calories from the Caesar cashew sauce. Win-win! As we know, some salads aren't as healthy as others, but this recipe qualifies as healthy, tasty, and delicious! I really love these homemade croutons; they're super crunchy and made with a lot less oil! You can use these croutons on soups or other fun salads.

INGREDIENTS

Salad
1 large head romaine lettuce
2–3 C lacinato kale

Dressing
¾ C cashews, soaked 2 hours
½ C water
Juice of half a lemon
1 Tbsp vegan mayonnaise
2 tsp maple syrup
2 tsp white wine vinegar
2 cloves of garlic
½ tsp salt
¼ tsp black pepper
A few grates of lemon zest
A few dashes of cayenne pepper

Croutons
Artisan bread, cut into small cubes
    (5–6 slices)
1 Tbsp olive oil
2 tsp nutritional yeast
½ tsp garlic powder
¼ tsp salt
A few dashes of black pepper

Topping
Pine nuts
Hemp seeds

DIRECTIONS

1. Clean and slice romaine lettuce into long strips. Same with kale.

2. Throw contents for dressing into a high-speed blender or Vitamix, and blend until perfectly smooth and creamy. If it's too thick for your liking, add 1–2 Tbsp of water.

3. For the croutons, toss bread with ingredients. Place in a toaster oven at 350 degrees for about 5 minutes.

4. Pour dressing over salad until well dressed, but not too much, since you don't want to weigh it down.

5. Top with croutons, hemp seeds, and pine nuts. Enjoy!

BLACKBERRY & GRAPEFRUIT SALAD WITH RASPBERRY VINAIGRETTE

SERVES

··· « 4 » ···

I love all sorts of salad combinations, and one of my favorite combos is fresh fruit or berries with peppery greens, like arugula. I also love adding quinoa or farro, which are high-fiber and protein-dense grains. Blackberries are high in antioxidants and anthocyanins, which have been found to boost memory function. Grapefruit contains the perfect balance of bitter, sweet, and sour. It is a very low-calorie fruit that strengthens the immune system and helps prevent insulin-resistance. The raspberry vinaigrette is a refreshing way to dress the bitter greens and fruit. You'll be mesmerized by the delightful flavors and textures of this salad!

INGREDIENTS

Salad
1 large grapefruit
1 6 oz pack blackberries
1 5 oz container arugula
Handful of toasted pine nuts

Farro
½ C Farro
1 C water
½ C vegetable stock
½ tsp salt

Raspberry vinaigrette
1 6 oz pack raspberries
½ C water
1 shallot
1 Tbsp white wine vinegar
2 tsp maple syrup
2 tsp olive oil
2 tsp lemon juice
1 ½ tsp salt
¼ tsp black pepper

Topping
Pine nuts

DIRECTIONS

1. Start with the farro. You can follow the instructions on your packet or do the following: Rinse using a colander, then place in a small pot with the water, vegetable stock, and salt on high heat. Once boiling, set to a simmer for about 35 minutes. Discard excess water and set aside to cool.

2. For the vinaigrette, throw all ingredients in food processor or high-speed blender. Blend until smooth.

3. For the salad, toss arugula with the farro. Peel and slice grapefruit. Top along with the blackberries and pine nuts.

4. Drizzle a generous amount of the raspberry vinaigrette and top with pine nuts. Enjoy!

FATTOUSH SALAD

SERVES
··· « 4 ~ 6 » ···

Growing up in Lebanon, I had the opportunity to explore a wide variety of culinary masterpieces that are typical everyday foods for most Lebanese. Fattoush is a zesty, earthy combination of vegetables topped with crispy pita chips, with a perfectly tart vinaigrette. The pita chips are traditionally fried, but here you can lightly spray oil on them and bake. One of the most unique things about fattoush is the spice we put in the vinaigrette that gives it the delicious tangy, lemony flavor. This spice is sumac. Sumac is a widely used spice in the Middle East. It comes in the form of berries that grow on a sumac bush. These berries are dried and then ground and used to flavor popular Lebanese dishes. Sumac is also known to have anti-inflammatory and cancer-fighting properties. Whether you're having sumac for its health benefits or for its tangy flavor, it's a spice you want to take advantage of, and Fattoush is one of the best avenues for its use!

INGREDIENTS

Salad
2 heads romaine lettuce, loosely chopped
3–4 Persian cucumbers, sliced
7–10 oz cherry tomatoes, halved
1 medium-sized red onion, julienned
1 can garbanzo beans
½ bunch fresh parsley, chopped
5–6 radishes, sliced

Vinaigrette
Juice of one lemon
1 ½ Tbsp olive oil
1 Tbsp white wine vinegar
2 tsp pomegranate molasses, or regular molasses
2 cloves of garlic, mashed
½ tsp sea salt, add more as desired
½ tsp sumac
a few dashes of black pepper

Pita chips
1–2 pitas, cut into squares

DIRECTIONS

1. After chopping veggies, toss in a large bowl and set aside.
2. Mix all ingredients for the vinaigrette in a small bowl.
3. Cut pita bread into roughly 1-inch squares and separate the parts. You can lightly spray the pita bread squares with oil. Toast in the oven for about 5–7 minutes at 350 degrees, until crispy chips form.
4. Add the dressing to the salad, toss, and top with crispy bread chips. Enjoy!

GARDEN POTATO SALAD

SERVES

···《 4 》···

Potato salad was one of my favorite foods growing up. I especially liked the salty pickle bits, which here I substituted with capers. Potato salad is a fun dish because you can add whatever veggies you like, and you can make it different every time. This elegant dish is very easy to put together and makes for a lovely potluck or dinner party option. Everyone loves their potato salad! This is, of course, a healthier version, so if you feel like it needs a bit more love, feel free to add more of whatever you think it needs. After all, these recipes are recommendations, not rules!

INGREDIENTS

Base

8–10 small red potatoes, skin on
1 ½ C celery, chopped
½ red onion, chopped
2–3 Tbsp capers
1–2 tsp vegetable oil

Dressing

¼ C veggie mayonnaise
3 Tbsp fresh dill, lightly chopped
2 Tbsp white wine vinegar
2 tsp maple syrup
1 tsp salt, add more as desired
¼ tsp black pepper

DIRECTIONS

1. Cut up potatoes into 1-inch pieces. Roast for 30–35 minutes at 350 degrees with vegetable oil. Then broil for about 5 minutes. Set aside to cool.

2. In a large bowl, place chopped celery, onion, and capers. Then add the potatoes and lightly toss.

3. For the dressing, mix ingredients in a small bowl with a fork until well incorporated. Pour over potato salad, and toss until well coated. Top with more capers if desired. Enjoy!

MEDITERRANEAN-STYLE BEET SALAD

SERVES
··· « 4 ∽ 6 » ···

When I was a little girl, I used to take pieces of my beet salad and rub it against my lips to make them red, since I wasn't allowed to play with makeup! Now, I've learned to like beets for more reasons than their cosmetic properties. Ha! Beets are among the most nutritionally endowed root vegetables, with high amounts of immune-boosting vitamin C, fiber, and essential minerals such as potassium and manganese. Another reason why I love beets is because they are super high in nitrates, which helps to boost your stamina by enhancing your body's use of oxygen! Through a nifty chain reaction, your body changes nitrates into nitric oxide, which helps regulate and improve blood flow. Studies have been conducted with athletes who were given beet juice prior to an endurance run and compared with a group that consumed berries instead. Athletes who received beet juice could run further, longer, and had lower blood pressure. Quite fascinating!

INGREDIENTS

3 large beets
1 bunch fresh parsley
Juice of half a lemon
1–2 cloves of garlic, mashed
1 Tbsp olive oil
1 Tbsp sesame seeds
½ tsp salt, or more as desired
A few dashes of black pepper

Garnish
Sesame seeds

DIRECTIONS

1. Steam beets for 1 hour until cooked through. Set aside to cool. Peel and cut into cubes.

2. Mix with chopped fresh parsley.

3. Smash garlic, and then add olive oil, lemon, sesame seeds, salt, and black pepper. Mix well.

4. Add to your beet salad. Mix thoroughly, and then sprinkle with sesame seeds. Enjoy!

Sandwiches

& Burgers

HAWAIIAN BURGER

MAKES
···« *6 large Patties* »···

You've probably heard of pineapple on pizza, but have you heard of pineapple on a burger? This Hawaiian version is everything you want in a juicy burger, from the sweetness of the grilled pineapple to the savory and umami flavors of the plant-based burger to the tangy-saltiness of the red cabbage sauerkraut packaged beautifully between two fluffy buns. The benefits of red cabbage are numerous: it is an immune booster, combats chronic diseases, promotes healthy bones, and improves gut health. Sauerkraut, which is essentially fermented cabbage, takes these existing benefits and adds the powerhouse effects of probiotics (good bacteria), which help to stabilize and improve your microbiome, which is largely your main source of immunity.

INGREDIENTS

6 oz cremini mushrooms
½ C walnuts
1 white onion
1 C short brown rice
¾ C almond flour
¼ C all-purpose flour
1 Tbsp vegetable oil

Spices and flavoring

2 Tbsp nutritional yeast
1 Tbsp barbecue sauce
1 Tbsp Worcestershire sauce
2 tsp brown sugar
1 tsp garlic powder
1 tsp cumin
2 tsp salt
¼ tsp black pepper

Trimmings

Vegan mayonnaise
Green leaf lettuce
Purple sauerkraut
Fresh pineapple, sliced, grilled
Alfalfa sprouts

Bread

Burger bun

DIRECTIONS

1. Slice the cremini mushrooms in quarters, then throw into a food processor. Lightly pulse until small chunks remain. Set aside.

2. Do the same with the walnuts, until small granules remain.

3. You can chop the onion or place in the food processor as well.

4. For the brown rice, follow cooking instructions on the package for one cup of dry rice. Once ready, set aside to cool, then place in the food processor until sticky consistency is formed. This will be used as the binder for the burgers.

5. In a skillet, pour 1 Tbsp of oil. Set to medium-high heat and sauté the mushroom, walnuts, and onion until cooked down (about 3 minutes). Set aside.

6. In a large bowl, incorporate the skillet contents with the almond flour, sticky brown rice, all-purpose flour, and the spices and flavoring ingredients. Use your hands to fully incorporate.

7. Lay parchment paper on a tray. Form about 3 ½-inch wide and a little over an 1-inch thick patties. Bake in the oven for about 35 minutes at 375 degrees. Set to broil for 5 min. Set aside to cool.

8. For the pineapple, slice, lightly oil, and grill using a grill pan until grill marks form.

9. Layer your burger as follows: mayonnaise, lettuce, the burger patty, pineapple, more lettuce, and top with sauerkraut and sprouts. Enjoy!

TOFU-RKY APPLE & WALNUT SANDWICH

SERVES

··· « 4 » ···

Who doesn't love a mouthwatering sandwich with juicy layers held between perfectly toasted slices of sourdough bread? I wanted to see if I could take tofu and mimic the sweet and savory flavors of turkey, and this was a pleasant result! I love incorporating fruit like apples with savory flavors; it has a way of elevating a dish. Granny Smith apples are especially high in fiber and vitamin C. Tofu is a great source of protein, contains iron, calcium, and eight essential amino acids. Putting these ingredients and trimmings together results in a pretty impressive sandwich that looks as good as it tastes.

INGREDIENTS

Tofu-rky strips
1 pack extra firm tofu
1 Tbsp soy sauce
1 Tbsp honey
2 tsp vegetable oil
½ tsp garlic powder
¼ tsp salt
A few dashes of black pepper

Walnut mayo
¼ C vegan mayonnaise
Handful of crushed walnuts
Handful of parsley, chopped
Black pepper and salt, to taste
Dash of cayenne pepper

Layer with
Arugula
Slices of Granny Smith apples
Alfalfa sprouts

Bread
Toasted sourdough slices

DIRECTIONS

1. For the tofu-rky strips, slice tofu into thin strips, marinate with soy sauce, honey, garlic powder, salt, and pepper. Let sit for a few minutes. Using a nonstick pan, lightly oil, and then lay strips to grill. Grill each side until caramelized and firm. Set aside to rest.

2. For the walnut mayo, mix in walnuts with mayo and parsley and add salt, pepper, and cayenne to taste.

3. Toast the bread in a toaster oven until golden brown.

4. Layer in this manner: spread walnut mayo on bread, lay sliced apples, then tofu-rky strips, followed by arugula and alfalfa sprouts, top with another slab of walnut mayo on bread. Press, slice, and serve! Enjoy!

JACKFRUIT WONDER BURGER

SERVES

···≪ 4 ≫···

For a second you might think this juicy burger was cradling a generous portion of pulled pork, but if you look again, you'll discover it is, in fact, good old jackfruit! Juicy, meaty, tasty, and loaded with flavor, this burger will surprise your taste buds and do your body some serious good! Aside from its unique flavor and meaty texture, jackfruit has an impressive nutritional profile. It is nutrient-dense, rich in fiber, and surprisingly high in protein. It can also be considered a "complete" food due to its balanced content of fat, protein, and carbohydrates. For vitamins and minerals, it is specifically rich in B complex vitamins, riboflavin, folic acid, iron, and magnesium. I will say it was quite the challenge photographing this one since all I wanted to do was dive into it!

INGREDIENTS

Jackfruit
2 cans jackfruit
4 Tbsp barbecue sauce
1 Tbsp vegetable oil
1 Tbsp honey
1 Tbsp apple cider vinegar
½ tsp garlic powder
½ tsp salt
¼ tsp black pepper
¼ tsp cayenne pepper (optional)

Potato wedges
7–8 baby purple potatoes, wedged
2 tsp vegetable oil
½ tsp garlic powder
½ tsp salt
¼ tsp black pepper

Cabbage slaw
2 C purple cabbage, shredded
1 Tbsp vegan mayonnaise
A squeeze of lemon juice
A few dashes of black pepper

Special sandwich sauce
4 Tbsp vegan mayonnaise
2 Tbsp tomato paste
¼ red onion, minced
1 Tbsp apple cider vinegar
1 Tbsp agave syrup
½ tsp salt
¼ tsp black pepper

Veggies
Lettuce leaves
White onion

Bread
Whole wheat burger bun, toasted

DIRECTIONS

1. Drain canned jackfruit. Place in a pot with water covering the top. Set to high heat until boiling. Boil for 2–3 minutes. Strain the jackfruit. Let cool.

2. Oil your pan. Set to medium-high heat. Marinate the jackfruit with the garlic powder, salt, and peppers, and cook for about 5 minutes.

3. Begin to pull apart and separate the chunks of jackfruit. Now, add the barbecue sauce, honey, and apple cider vinegar, and simmer on medium-low heat for 15 minutes, stirring occasionally.

4. In the meantime, prep your cabbage slaw, veggies and potato wedges. For cabbage slaw, mix ingredients in a bowl, set aside. For the veggies, wash and slice, set aside. For the potato wedges, toss your potato wedges into a bowl with the oil and seasonings, transfer to a pan lined with parchment paper or foil and place in an oven at 400 degrees for about 30–35 minutes or until baked through and golden brown.

5. For the sandwich sauce, in a small bowl, mix all the ingredients until incorporated.

6. Once your jackfruit is ready, scoop a generous portion on to the buns while hot. Top with slaw and veggies and Special Sandwich Sauce, and you're good to go! Enjoy!

PAPRIKA GARBANZO & ZESTY POTATO WRAPS

SERVES
···«4»···

If you're looking for a fun way to prepare your garbanzo beans, then try this! Garbanzo beans are wonderfully versatile legumes. They're high in protein and can be incorporated in soups, as a spread, or, in this case, a scrumptious layer in a wrap. When I was living in Lebanon, there was a delicious sandwich my dad used to pick up for us as kids from a mom-and-pop shop on the road back home that basically was a large pita bread lined with fries, pickles, cabbage, and a potent garlic sauce. It was wrapped into what I can only describe now as a massive burrito. So essentially this wrap is a spin on that childhood memory, only less greasy and much healthier!

INGREDIENTS

Paprika garbanzos
2 cans garbanzo beans
1 Tbsp tomato paste
2 tsp paprika
1 Tbsp nutritional yeast
1 Tbsp vegetable oil
1 tsp garlic powder
1 tsp salt
A few dashes black pepper
A few dashes of cayenne pepper

Zesty potato wedges
4 medium golden potatoes
1 Tbsp lemon zest
1 Tbsp vegetable oil
1 Tbsp lemon juice
½ tsp salt
¼ tsp ground pepper

Sauce
Special Sandwich Sauce recipe
  (see recipe on page 135)

Veggies
Avocado slices
Baby spinach
Vine tomatoes
Microgreens

Bread
Whole wheat lavash bread

DIRECTIONS

1. For the paprika garbanzos, drain garbanzo beans and lightly rinse in a colander. Marinate with assigned ingredients. Set aside.

2. For the potatoes, slice into strips about half an inch thick. Marinate with assigned ingredients. Set aside.

3. Place garbanzo beans on parchment paper on a tray. If it's large enough, add the potatoes. If not, do the same with the potatoes on another tray.

4. Place in the oven set to 375 degrees for 30 minutes. Then set to broil for about 10–15 at 400 degrees. Keep an eye on them to prevent burning.

5. Once ready, pull out of the oven and set aside to cool.

6. Spread the Special Sandwich Sauce on your lavash bread. Line with avocado slices, tomato, spinach, and microgreens. Then add potato slices and the garbanzos. Mash down the garbanzos into the bread (it will help it roll up nicely). Once done, roll like a burrito, slice, and serve. Enjoy!

"MOZZARELLA" ARTICHOKE PANINIS

SERVES
···《 4 》···

How mouthwatering does this look? This recipe was a surprise waiting to happen! I was a little blown away when my plant-based mozzarella began behaving like real melted cheese! I really like mozzarella, but not so much the dairy part, since I'm mildly lactose intolerant. This sandwich gave me everything I wanted in a gooey melted cheese experience, without any cheese in sight! The mozzarella is super easy to make and mainly made out of cashews, nutritional yeast, and tapioca. Tapioca is the starchy substance obtained from the cassava root, which is native to Brazil. This sandwich right here is nothing short of a real treat!

INGREDIENTS

"Mozzarella"
½ C raw cashews, soaked 2 hours
2 C water
3 Tbsp tapioca powder
2 Tbsp nutritional yeast
1 Tbsp lemon juice
1 tsp onion powder
1 tsp garlic powder
1 tsp salt
1 tsp sugar
A few dashes of black pepper

Trimmings
Marinated artichoke hearts
Sun-dried tomatoes, sliced
Fresh basil, sliced
Alfalfa sprouts

Bread
Whole wheat loaf (you can also
   use ciabatta bread)

DIRECTIONS

1. Throw all ingredients for your "mozzarella" into a Vitamix or high-speed blender. Blend until smooth and incorporated. Pour into a small pot and continuously stir using a spatula on medium-high heat until boiling. Once boiling, set to medium heat and continue to stir. You will notice it will become thick and sticky, like melted mozzarella. At this point, remove from heat, cover with the lid, and set aside.

2. Place a generous portion of the "mozzarella" on the bread, and top with artichoke, sun-dried tomatoes, fresh basil strips, and sprouts. You can add another layer of your cheese, and then press your bread on to it.

3. Place sandwich on a grill skillet, or a panini press, and grill each side for about 2 minutes.

4. Remove from heat and slice. Enjoy!

Note: You can use this mozzarella recipe in a variety of other dishes, such as onion soup, pizza, and lasagna!

PORTOBELLO MUSHROOM BURGER WITH MANGO SLAW

SERVES

⋯《 3–4 Burgers 》⋯

This burger is simply amazing. Crispy layer on the outside, and a perfectly cooked meaty texture on the inside. Mushrooms have to be one of my favorite things to eat! I just love the beautiful umami flavors it gives off when cooked, and how well it compliments different dishes. Some foods you need to really work with to bring out their characteristic flavors, but mushrooms seem to have an effortless charm to them that is easy to harness and enjoyably satisfying to indulge in. These burgers are a fantastic option for a fun dinner party with friends, and hit the spot every time.

INGREDIENTS

3–4 portobello mushrooms

Pre-battering
½ C flour

Batter
¾ C non-sweetened almond milk
½ C flour
2 tsp nutritional yeast
1 tsp cornstarch
½ tsp salt
1 tsp garlic powder
¼ tsp black pepper

Bread crumbs
½ C bread crumbs
1 tsp dried parsley
½ tsp salt
½ tsp garlic or onion powder

Mango slaw
1 C chopped mango
2 C shredded purple cabbage
½ C chopped fresh parsley
3 Tbsp vegan mayonnaise
1 Tbsp white wine vinegar
¼ tsp salt, add more to taste
A few dashes of black pepper

Burger bun
Brioche or whole wheat
(lightly toast the inside of your bun)

Layer with arugula

DIRECTIONS

1. Lightly clean your mushroom under running water. In a bowl, place the flour, then toss your mushroom and make sure it is completely covered with the flour. Dust off any excess. Set aside. Repeat with the rest.

2. In another bowl, mix in the ingredients for the batter. Set aside.

3. For the bread crumbs, do the same.

4. Set your oven to bake at 375 degrees.

5. When ready, place your flour-covered mushrooms in the batter. Using tongs, remove, and then cover with your bread-crumb mix. Repeat with the rest.

6. Using spray oil, lightly spray your mushrooms, top and bottom.

7. Line a baking tray with parchment paper. Place your mushrooms with the bottom down for the first 15 minutes. Then flip them over for another 15 minutes or so. Once done, flip them again and set to broil for about 5–7 minutes. Remove from the oven and place on a cooling rack.

8. While waiting for it to cool and crisp, mix all mango slaw ingredients.

9. Build your burger as follows: bun, arugula, breaded mushroom, mango slaw, more arugula, and top with your bun. Enjoy!

Note: You can use an air fryer instead of the oven if you have one, just set to 375 degrees and air fry your battered mushrooms for about 20–25 minutes.

TOFU BLT

SERVES
···« 3 ~ 4 sandwiches »···

I've spoken about tofu quite a lot, but it really is a conveniently versatile food that is a good source of protein and contains all nine of the essential amino acids! Here we're taking our humble tofu and transforming it into fun bacon strips that you can throw in sandwiches. They're easy to make and taste great between toasted bread with all of your favorite sandwich trimmings. Kids will especially like it, and it's a lot healthier than the packaged artificial meats, since they don't have any preservatives or unwanted chemicals, aside from your basic and easy to prepare marinade.

INGREDIENTS

Tofu
1 pack extra-firm tofu

Tofu marinade
2 Tbsp soy sauce
1 Tbsp maple syrup
1 Tbsp vegetable oil
1 tsp onion powder
½ tsp garlic powder
¼ tsp black pepper

Mayo sauce
¼ C vegan mayonnaise
¼ a red onion, minced
3 Tbsp capers, minced
2 tsp white wine vinegar
¼ tsp salt
A few dashes of black pepper

Veggies
Tomatoes
Lettuce
Red onion

Bread
Toasted whole-grain bread

DIRECTIONS

1. Slice your tofu block into thin strips. Mix the marinade ingredients in a small bowl. Pour over the tofu, and let sit for 10–15 minutes before cooking.

2. Lightly oil a nonstick pan and set to medium-high heat. Place the strips in the pan, and cook until golden brown (3–5 minutes). Then flip over and cook the other side.

3. Mix the ingredients for the mayo sauce.

4. Toast the bread and spread the sauce. Build the sandwich starting with the lettuce, two layers of tofu bacon, tomato, red onion, and another layer of lettuce. Top with bread. Enjoy!

HOMEMADE BAKED FALAFEL

SERVES

···« 20 ¼"-cup Falafel »···

Growing up in Lebanon, I had the opportunity to have some of the best falafel sandwiches in the world, literally! Falafel happens to be completely plant-based, which is great! However, traditionally falafel is deep-fried. Here I tried baking them to make it lighter and easier on the gut. It turned out quite delicious! What really pulls a good falafel sandwich together is the tahini sauce, which is essentially made out of hulled and ground sesame seeds, a powerhouse of nutrients and minerals. I like to add fresh parsley and lots of garlic to it, which gives more depth and flavor!

INGREDIENTS

Falafel
1 lb dried garbanzo beans, soaked
   overnight
1 bunch of fresh parsley
½ C water
½ large white onion
3 Tbsp vegetable oil
2 Tbsp flour
3 tsp salt
3 tsp cumin
1 ½ tsp baking powder
½ tsp black pepper
2–3 cloves of garlic
A few dashes of cayenne pepper

Tahini sauce
¼ C tahini
¼ C water
2 cloves of garlic, mashed
A handful of parsley, minced
1 Tbsp lemon juice
1 Tbsp white wine vinegar
¼ tsp salt
A few dashes of black pepper

Trimmings
Whole wheat pita bread
Red onion
Tomato
Lettuce

DIRECTIONS

1. You'll notice after soaking your garbanzo beans overnight that they will have doubled, if not tripled, in size. Depending on how big your food processor is, you can either divide all the ingredients into two sections, or get it done in one batch.

2. Dissolve the baking powder in the ½ C of water, cut your onion into large chunks and roughly chop your parsley. Then throw all falafel ingredients into your food processor, and continue to process until fully incorporated. When the texture is partly grainy and formable, it should be ready to bake.

3. Set your oven to 375 degrees. Line a baking tray with parchment paper and spray with cooking oil. Using a ¼ measuring cup, pack your falafel mix. Then, using your hands, form mix into falafel discs. You can also form them into balls, but I prefer this shape since it's easier to fit into a pita pocket. Once done, spray the top of the falafels with your cooking oil.

4. Place in the oven for about 25–30 minutes, until the top turns golden brown.

5. Set aside to cool.

6. For the tahini sauce, place all ingredients in a small bowl and mix until incorporated. If you would like thicker or thinner sauce, decrease or increase the water.

7. Slice your pita in half, forming two pockets. Line with lettuce, onion, tomato, and then the falafel. Drizzle the tahini sauce. Enjoy!

appetizer

& Sides

SPINACH PIES

MAKES
··· « 14 ~ 16 Pies » ···

This is where spinach meets dough in one of the most beautiful ways! The flavor order you're going to experience is earthy spinach mingled with savory onion and hints of lemon, enveloped in the sweetness of the dough. The lemon causes your mouth to water, which releases an enzyme called salivary amylase. This enzyme changes the starch in the dough to maltose, and thus literally enhances your ability to taste the sweetness present. And there you have it, a beautiful balance of sweet, sour, and savory! You don't need me to tell you the numerous benefits of spinach. I hope you enjoy it!

INGREDIENTS

Dough
3 C all-purpose flour
⅓ C vegetable oil
2 Tbsp olive oil
1 tsp active dry yeast
1 tsp sugar
1 C warm water
1 tsp salt

Filling
8 C fresh spinach, or 2 lbs frozen
 spinach, thawed, drained, and
 squeezed dry
1 ½ C yellow onion, finely diced
½ tsp black pepper
⅓ C pine nuts
1 Tbsp vegetable oil
1 tsp salt
¼ tsp black pepper
¼ C lemon juice

DIRECTIONS

Dough
1. Proof the yeast by dissolving it in ¼ cup of the warm water with the sugar and letting it activate for about 10 minutes. Whisk flour and salt together in a mixing bowl.
2. Add the oils and mix into the dough. Now add the remaining warm water slowly. Add more of the water as necessary to create a sticky dough.
3. Knead by hand until the dough is soft and smooth.
4. Cover with plastic wrap and let rise in a warm spot until doubled, about 90 minutes.

Forming the triangles
1. Combine and mix the ingredients for the filling.
2. Roll half of the dough out on a dry work surface to ⅛-inch thickness. Cut dough into 4-inch rounds.
3. Fill the rounds of dough by placing a heaping tablespoon of spinach mix in the center of each round. Place a few pine nuts on top of the filling.
4. Bring three sides of the dough together in the center over the filling, and pinch into a triangle. Close the dough firmly.

Bake
5. Preheat the oven to 375 degrees. Place the pies on baking sheets, and brush or spray the dough with olive oil.
6. Bake for 18–20 minutes, or until golden brown.
7. Set the oven to broil for the last 5 minutes of baking to increase browning.
8. Once done, remove from oven and let cool. Dust a little flour on them, and store in an airtight container. Can last up to a week in the fridge.

FUSION LETTUCE WRAP

SERVES
··· « 4 » ···

The first time I presented these wraps to my then fiancé, inspired by a fusion of Asian flavors, I was pleasantly surprised when he mumbled with a half-full mouth and side smile: "This is my favorite dish you've ever made." I've since had it grace our table on several occasions and family dinners! And, well, what's not to love? The punch of ginger, saltiness of the soy sauce, nuttiness of peanut butter, and sweetness of raw honey coming together with bits of tofu, carrots, onion, and the crunch of roasted almonds, enveloped in a crisp, cool bite of butter lettuce, need I say more?

INGREDIENTS

Stuffing
1 block extra firm tofu
5 medium-sized carrots
1 medium yellow onion
½ C roasted almonds, crushed
1 inch fresh ginger, minced
2 tsp sesame seeds
2 Tbsp soy sauce
1 Tbsp vegetable oil
½ tsp salt + a few dashes of black
   pepper and cayenne pepper

Peanut sauce
⅓ C water
¼ C all-natural peanut butter
3 Tbsp soy sauce
1 Tbsp of raw honey
1 Tbsp of vegetable oil
1 inch fresh ginger, minced
2 cloves of garlic, minced
Juice of one lime
Dash of cayenne pepper

Wrap
Fresh butter lettuce leaves

DIRECTIONS

1. Chop tofu into small cubes, then toss into heated pan with vegetable oil, ginger, and soy sauce. Set heat to medium-high. After about 4–5 minutes, add the chopped carrots and onion. Cook for 10–15 minutes on medium heat, turning frequently. Wait till onion is partly golden, then add black pepper, cayenne, and salt, as desired. Once cooked, add the crushed almonds and sesame seeds.

2. For the peanut sauce, mix contents thoroughly in a bowl.

3. Spoon stuffing mix into butter lettuce leaves, and drizzle peanut sauce. Enjoy!

MUSHROOM-STUFFED ZUCCHINI BOATS

SERVES

··· « 3 ⌣ 4 » ···

This appetizer is one my family's favorites! It has several layers of Italian flavors, from the meaty mushrooms and red onions to the sun-dried tomatoes and fresh basil. Zucchinis have been shown to aid in maintaining weight loss and improving heart health, digestion, and eye health. They contains phytonutrients such as lutein and beta-carotene, which is converted into vitamin A in the body. This antiaging food is one of the most versatile of vegetables and can be used in everything from raw zucchini noodles to warm zucchini bread!

INGREDIENTS

4–5 medium-sized zucchinis

1 pack cremini mushrooms

½ large red onion, brunoised

¼ C sun-dried tomatoes, brunoised

¼ C fresh basil, minced

½ C raw cashews

2 Tbsp seasoned bread crumbs

2 Tbsp olive oil

½ tsp salt

¼ tsp black pepper

DIRECTIONS

1. Prep veggies. Chop cremini mushrooms into small pieces. Place raw cashews in the food processor until granule-sized pieces form. Cut off the ends of the zucchini, then slice in half. Scrape out the inside using a spoon to about ½ an inch for the boat's thickness. Lightly dab with olive oil. Place in the oven at 325 degrees for 10 minutes. Remove, then set aside.

2. In a bowl mix the remaining contents.

3. Spoon contents into the boats, and pile contents up.

4. Place back in the oven on broil for another 10 minutes at 325 degrees. Remove and serve. Enjoy!

HASSELBACK POTATOES WITH ROASTED GARLIC SAUCE

SERVES

···《 4 》···

Hasselback potatoes take the humble baked potato to a whole new level. It's the perfect balance of rustic and elegant. The roasted garlic sauce is simply superb and brings so much character and life to these potatoes. This is definitely one of my favorite appetizers, and it's so easy to make! I hope you enjoy it.

INGREDIENTS

Potatoes
12–16 baby red potatoes
1 Tbsp olive oil
½ tsp ground rosemary
¼ tsp salt
¼ tsp black pepper

Roasted garlic sauce
¾ C raw cashews,
   soaked for 2 hours
1 C water
1 head roasted garlic
1 Tbsp olive oil
2 tsp maple syrup
2 raw cloves of garlic
2 tsp white wine vinegar
1 tsp salt
¼ tsp black pepper
A few dashes of cayenne pepper

Toppings
Chopped parsley, green onion,
   or thyme

DIRECTIONS

1. For the potatoes, clean, then cut even, thin slices, stopping at about ¼-inch from the bottom. Repeat with all potatoes.

2. Place olive oil, rosemary, salt, and black pepper on a small plate, and use a cooking brush to lightly dab the top of the potatoes.

3. Take the head of garlic and slice it from its side across, exposing the inside.

4. Brush a little olive oil into the exposed garlic sides, and add a few dashes of salt and pepper.

5. Roast in the oven for about 20–25 minutes at 375 degrees, or until cooked through. Then broil for about 5 minutes, until golden brown edges form.

6. In a blender, add the roasted garlic (you should be able to easily squeeze them out of the skin), cashews, water, and remaining ingredients, and blend until perfectly smooth.

7. Drizzle over baked potatoes, and add desired topping. Enjoy!

NUTTY SUMMER ROLLS

SERVES
··· « 6 ~ 8 » ···

One of my favorite things about summer rolls is that they are extremely satisfying and high in nutrients, and yet light in calories! Paired with a savory peanut sauce high in electrolytes, protein, and essential oils, it's hard to imagine something this tasty could count as part of a healthy diet plan. The peanut sauce contains sesame oil, which has antibacterial and anti-inflammatory properties. It's also rich in several minerals, such as calcium and magnesium. These summer rolls can act as an appetizer, lunch, or light dinner option.

INGREDIENTS

1 pack rice paper
1 pack vermicelli rice noodles
2 heads organic butter lettuce
2 medium-sized ripe avocados
1 pack shredded carrots
1 pack bean sprouts
1 package extra-firm tofu (+ 2 tsp
    soy sauce + 2 tsp honey)
1 pack crispy seaweed strips

Peanut sauce

¼ C soy sauce
3 Tbsp all-natural peanut butter
2 Tbsp rice vinegar
2 Tbsp sesame oil
2–3 Tbsp water
2 tsp sriracha sauce
1 tsp garlic, minced
1 tsp ginger, minced

DIRECTIONS

1. For the tofu, lightly oil a nonstick pan. Slice tofu block into ¼-inch thick slices, then cut each slice into two pieces to form strips. Marinate with a little soy sauce and honey. Let sit, then add to hot pan and sauté until caramelized edges appear. Set aside to cool.

2. For the vermicelli rice noodles, follow the instructions on your packet. Once ready, run under cold water in a colander, and set aside.

3. To form the spring rolls, pour hot water on a deep, flat dish. Dip rice paper for a few seconds, then remove once soft. Spread out on a cutting board. Prep veggies, then line veggies in the center starting with butter lettuce and top other veggies and avocado as desired. Gently find the ends, fold in sides, and roll tightly, like you would a burrito. Slice in the middle.

4. For the peanut sauce, thoroughly mix all contents together using a whisk. Dip in spring rolls. Enjoy!

GARLIC-ROASTED VEGGIE KEBABS

MAKES
···« 10~12 Kebabs »···

Roasted vegetables are simply the best! In this recipe, I have baby purple potatoes, cherry tomatoes on the vine, zucchini, and cremini mushrooms with loads of garlic. Most of the health benefits coming from garlic are because of a sulfuric compound that is released when garlic is crushed, chopped, or chewed. It's called allicin, and it's what gives garlic its potent smell and flavor. Allicin has been shown in clinical studies to reduce total cholesterol and increase HDL. It's also been found to restore suppressed antibody response and even has antimicrobial properties. I like to think about it as flavorful medicine!

INGREDIENTS

Garlic dipping sauce
½ C raw cashews, soaked 2 hours
½ C water
4–5 cloves of garlic
2 Tbsp vegan mayonnaise
1 Tbsp white wine vinegar
Juice of ½ a lemon
½ tsp salt
A few dashes of cayenne pepper

Vegetable marinade
2 cloves of garlic, mashed
1 stem rosemary, ground
¼ tsp salt
A few dashes of black pepper
1–2 Tbsp vegetable oil

Veggies
3 zucchinis
1 pack cremini mushrooms
1 head large garlic cloves
1 bunch cherry tomatoes
1 ½–2 lbs baby purple potatoes

DIRECTIONS

1. Drain cashews, then throw them into Vitamix or high-speed blender with remaining ingredients. Blend until creamy.

2. For the veggie marinade, mash garlic and grind rosemary in a mortar. Add oil, salt, and pepper.

3. After prepping your vegetables, place potatoes on a tray in the oven first for 15 minutes at 375 degrees, since it will take longer for them to cook. Set aside.

4. Skewer your veggies in desired order, and lightly dab marinate using a brush. Place veggie kebabs in the oven and bake for 15–20 minutes at 400 degrees. Then set to broil for another 5 minutes.

5. Once done, enjoy with garlic dipping sauce.

CASHEW-HONEY HERBED POTATO WEDGES

SERVES

···« 4 ～ 5 »···

I like to think about potatoes as the bread of the soil. It is a gluten-free, starchy vegetable that is packed full of energy, acts as a great source of potassium, and is mild in taste, which allows for controlled flavoring. Raw cashews are a wonderful option to create the tasty consistency that cheese can give off. Along with the aromatic flavors of dill and rosemary, the savory blend of garlic, salt, and pepper, topped with the caramelized sweetness of raw honey, balanced with the tartness of lemon zest, well let's just say it tastes as good as it looks!

INGREDIENTS

4–5 medium-sized potatoes, wedged

Potato wedge mix

½ C cashews

3 Tbsp vegetable oil

2 Tbsp raw honey

Juice of ½ a lemon

2 Tbsp flour

1 tsp garlic powder

1 tsp salt

2 strips fresh dill, chopped

1 strip fresh rosemary, chopped

1 tsp lemon zest

¼ tsp cracked black pepper

Topping

Green scallions, chopped

DIRECTIONS

1. Set oven to 400 degrees.

2. In a large bowl, toss the wedged potatoes with the flour. Set aside for a few minutes.

3. Toss the cashews in a food processor and pulse until grainy. In a small bowl, combine the granulated cashews, along with the remaining ingredients of the Potato Wedge Mix.

4. Now dress your potatoes with this mixture and let sit for 10 minutes or so before placing in the oven.

5. Line a baking tray with parchment paper. Place potato wedges upright on skin base to allow to cook on all sides. Bake about 30–35 minutes. Then set to broil for about 5 minutes. Watch closely to prevent burning.

6. Top with fresh green scallions. Enjoy!

Note: You can also create these wedges using an air fryer. Just set heat to 360 degrees for 35 minutes, tossing 2–3 times throughout the cooking time.

HUMMUS DONE RIGHT

SERVES
···« 6 ⁓ 8 »···

Being part Lebanese, I always thought hummus to be a deliciously simple recipe, but many are the times I questioned why it didn't quite taste right at that fancy restaurant or from that gourmet market. That's why I called this recipe Hummus Done Right! Sure, you can tweak it to your preference, but this recipe is what I have found to bring happiness to my soul! Garbanzo beans, also known as chickpeas, are loaded with muscle-building protein, dietary fiber, magnesium, potassium, and iron. An important part of hummus is tahini, which is toasted, ground, and hulled sesame seeds. Tahini is also packed with protein and contains calcium and copper, which are bone- and collagen-building minerals! So, what do you say? Shall we get hummus right, every time? Yes!

INGREDIENTS

Hummus
2 cans chickpeas,
    drained and rinsed
⅓ C Tahini
¼–½ C water
Juice of 1 whole lemon
2–3 cloves of garlic
1 tsp salt

Toppings
Chopped parsley
Olive oil
A few dashes of cayenne pepper

Hummus Pita Pockets
Pita bread
Baby arugula
Cherry tomatoes
Kalamata olives

DIRECTIONS

1. Throw the ingredients for your hummus into a food processor. If it's too thick, continue to add a little water until desired consistency is reached.

2. Spread into pita bread and add cherry tomatoes, Kalamata olives, and arugula, or use as a dip with pita chips or tortilla chips.

3. Top with olive oil, parsley, and cayenne pepper. Enjoy!

BABA GHANOUSH

···《 *Makes a medium—sized plate* 》···

You might have noticed my Lebanese side coming through a few times in these recipes. Here's another one of my favorites, baba ghanoush! This is an ancient recipe that has been handed down for generations in the Middle East, and, not to be biased, but I think I might have one of the best out there! It also helps that it is actually super easy to make. The smoked flavors of eggplant roasted on an open flame marry beautifully with the tartness of lemon, and the savory hints of garlic accentuated by sea salt and cayenne pepper add that much-loved sharpness, which is enveloped in the rich and nutty creaminess of the tahini. If you're looking for an exotic way to prepare your eggplants, then look no further. Enjoy!

INGREDIENTS

2 large eggplants
¼ C tahini
Juice of half a lemon
3 cloves of garlic
1 tsp salt
A few dashes of cayenne pepper

Pita chips
Pita bread, toasted

Toppings
Kalamata olives
Tomatoes
Parsley
Olive oil

DIRECTIONS

1. Roast your eggplants whole on an open flame until chard on the outside and soft on the inside. Set aside to cool for a few minutes, then remove the skin.

2. Using a fork, mash up your eggplants until you're left with a chunky consistency. Add your tahini, lemon, garlic, and salt, and mix until well incorporated. (Note: You can also throw all the ingredients in a food processor and pulse, but using a fork is the more authentic way of preparing it.)

3. Refrigerate for 1 hour.

4. Pita chips: Cut pita bread into small triangles. Separate joined pieces, and toast in the oven until crispy.

5. Remove baba ghanoush from fridge. Spread on a plate, and drizzle with olive oil and style as desired using toppings. Dip and enjoy!

CILANTRO POTATOES

SERVES

···« 4 ⌣ 6 »···

Native to Lebanese cuisine, this cilantro-covered potato dish makes for a delicious side that is traditionally served as part of the authentic Lebanese spread called meza. Meza can be described as a series of beautifully prepared "mini plates" that are shared by a family or group of friends. Believe it or not, I'm not a fan of fresh cilantro, but I absolutely love these potatoes. That's because when you cook or bake cilantro, the enzyme that I'm sensitive to is deactivated. So whether you like cilantro or not, this dish will not disappoint!

INGREDIENTS

5–6 medium golden potatoes
½ bunch fresh cilantro
4–5 cloves of garlic, mashed
1 ½ Tbsp vegetable oil
1 ½ tsp salt
½ tsp black pepper
A few dashes of cayenne pepper

Serve with ketchup (optional)

DIRECTIONS

1. Peel potatoes and cut into ½-inch cubes.

2. Chop cilantro and mix with oil, crushed garlic, salt, and pepper.

3. Set oven to 375 degrees. Marinate potatoes with cilantro mix. Spread onto parchment paper on a pan. Bake in the oven for 30–35 minutes. Then set to broil at 400 degrees for about 5 minutes, until golden-brown edges appear. Make sure to keep an eye on it to protect from burning. Set aside to cool. Once cooled, remove from parchment paper (should come right off with a spatula). Enjoy!

TOFU SALAD BRUSCHETTA

MAKES
···« 6 – 8 Bruschettas »···

Tofu is super versatile and easy to work with. This tofu salad bruschetta is the perfect quick breakfast or lunch option that is refreshing, satisfying, and low in calories. This could also be a great picnic or to-go lunch option since it's easy to pack and put together. What's giving the tofu the actual egg salad color is the tumeric, which also happens to be a fantastic anti-inflammatory agent. And yes, you have a complete meal here with all your macros!

INGREDIENTS

Tofu salad
1 pack firm tofu,
   drained and pressed
1 C celery, chopped
½ C parsley, chopped
3 Tbsp vegan mayonnaise
1 Tbsp nutritional yeast
2 tsp Dijon mustard
2 tsp turmeric
1 tsp salt
½ tsp onion powder
¼ tsp black pepper
A few dashes of cayenne pepper

Toppings
Artisan bread
Sriracha
Fresh spinach (or arugula)
Baby greens

DIRECTIONS

1. Drain tofu by pressing it and discarding fluid. Aside from the water in the container, you should be able to continue to drain up to ⅓ C fluid from the tofu block. When done, take a large bowl and break up tofu. Add celery and parsley. Mix in remaining ingredients. Press and mix with a large fork until well incorporated.

2. Toast bread in toaster oven for about 5 minutes at 350 degrees. Dollop a generous portion of the tofu salad onto your bread. Top with sriracha, spinach, and baby greens. You can also use arugula if you prefer. Enjoy!

SPICY MANGO SALSA

MAKES
···《 2~3 Cups 》···

I love anything with mango, so to me, this salsa is out of this world! It has so many delightful layers of flavor and offers you the perfect balance of a little sweet, a little tart, and a lot of heat! If you're looking for a fun way to prepare a unique appetizer with a Mexican flare, then this is it. You can even add this to some homemade tacos or use it as a topping on your favorite salad.

INGREDIENTS

2 partly ripe mangos
1 green bell pepper
1 red bell pepper
½ red onion
2–3 Tbsp cilantro
1 small jalapeño, minced
Juice of one lime
1 tsp white wine vinegar
½–1 tsp salt
A few dashes of cayenne pepper

Pair with black bean or corn chips

DIRECTIONS

1. Chop mangos and veggies uniformly. Place in a bowl.

2. If you don't want it to be too spicy, remove the seeds from the jalapeño. Mix in remaining ingredients. Serve with tortilla chips (the ones photographed here are black bean tortilla chips). Enjoy!

GUACAMOLE

MAKES

...« Approx. 2 Cups »...

I'm unapologetically obsessed with avocados. There was a time when all my husband and I would have for dinner nights in a row was guacamole on toasted artisan bread. There are so many different ways of making good guacamole! You can add tomatoes, onions, and salsa. You can make it chunky or creamy. Throw in some jalapeños to make it extra spicy, or make it perfectly mild. So, I wanted to go a little simpler with this recipe to offer you the opportunity to add whatever you think it needs to make it your own. Don't get me wrong, though, this recipe is nothing less than what I believe classic guacamole should be!

INGREDIENTS

3 medium ripe avocados
2–3 Tbsp cilantro
2 Tbsp lemon juice
3 cloves of garlic, mashed
2 tsp white wine vinegar
½ tsp salt, add more as desired
A few dashes of black pepper
A few dashes of cayenne pepper

Pair with black bean or corn chips

DIRECTIONS

1. Use a fork to mash avocados. Add ingredients while mixing and mashing.

2. Use a mortar and pestle to mash your garlic and mix into guacamole.

3. Serve with black bean or corn chips. Enjoy!

CORN BREAD

MAKES

···« 8x8—inch Pan »···

When I was a little girl, I remember one of my favorite things to have at our go-to family restaurant was freshly baked corn bread with honey. It was so good! I know now it wasn't the healthiest food to indulge in since corn bread usually has a lot of sugar and fat hidden in it. So I wanted to create a healthier version of one of my favorite childhood classics. I hope you enjoy it!

INGREDIENTS

Dry

1 C flour

1 C cornmeal

2 Tbsp flaxseed meal

4 tsp baking powder

2 Tbsp brown sugar

½ tsp salt

Wet

1 can full-fat coconut milk

½ C almond milk

6 Tbsp warm water

½ can sweet corn (optional)

1/3 C vegetable oil

2 Tbsp maple syrup

1 tsp apple cider vinegar

½ tsp vanilla

Serve with:

Honey

Chili beans

DIRECTIONS

1. Microwave the 6 Tbsp of water for 30 seconds. Add the flaxseed, and mix until thickened, about 2 minutes. Set aside.

2. Mix wet ingredients in a small bowl. Mix dry ingredients in a larger bowl. Once incorporated, add wet ingredients to dry ingredients and mix. Then add the flaxseed mixture. Do not over mix the batter, just until ingredients are incorporated.

3. Set your oven to 375 degrees. Spray oil your pan and pour in the batter. Bake for 25–30 minutes, or until you can poke it with a knife, and it comes out clean. Serve with honey or as a side with homemade chili beans. Enjoy!

HOMEMADE TORTILLAS

MAKES
····« 16 *Tortillas* »····

There's nothing quite like homemade fresh tortillas! I love tortillas, but most are made with animal fat and are quite high in calories. So, I decided to create a recipe that is higher in nutrients, free of animal fats, lighter, and just as delicious! One-third of the flour used here is actually almond flour, so even though there's still calories, they are what we call nutrient-dense calories, meaning you get the energy plus vitamins and nutrients!

INGREDIENTS

Flour tortillas
2 C all-purpose flour
1 C almond flour
3 Tbsp vegetable oil
1 tsp brown sugar
1 tsp salt
1 C warm water
1 tsp baking powder
A few dashes of cinnamon

DIRECTIONS

1. Using a bowl, mix in the dry ingredients. Then add the oil and use your hands to work the flour into the oil. Now, add the warm water and continue to work into the dough. After mixing for a minute, you'll notice the dough getting sticky. At this point, dust your kitchen counter with flour and start kneading the dough for at least 3–5 minutes. You can continue to dust a little more flour until you're done.

2. Now, slice your dough right down the middle, then again to create four pieces. Mound each piece, and repeat the sectioning until you get a total of 16 equal pieces. Wet your hands slightly, and roll each section into a ball.

3. Dust a little flour on parchment paper, and roll your tortillas directly on the parchment paper to about 7 inches wide.

4. Using a cast-iron skillet (if you don't have one, you can use a regular nonstick pan), set to medium-high heat. Once hot, flip the tortilla directly on to the skillet, with the parchment paper still attached and side up. After about 15–20 seconds, the parchment paper should peel off nicely. Give it a minute or so to cook on one side, until golden brown spots form. Flip, and do the other side.

5. After each tortilla is done, place in an airtight container to maintain its moisture.

6. You can use these tortillas to make some amazing tacos or quesadillas. Enjoy!

Des

erts

PLANT-BASED SNICKERS

MAKES
··«*20~24 Bars*»··

Every so often you make something that makes you so happy you wonder what your life would have been like without it. I chose to open the dessert section with my all-time favorite sweet treat! Since I was a child, the classic Snickers bar was king of all candy bars to me. Naturally, a plant-based version had to be in the works for this cookbook. I give you the best Snickers bar I've ever eaten, only this one contains no added sugar and does your body some real good!

INGREDIENTS

Base
1 C raw almonds, soaked 2 hours
½ C cashews, soaked 2 hours
¼ C coconut cream
¼ C water
2 Tbsp maple syrup
1 Tbsp coconut oil
¼ tsp salt

Caramel layer
12–14 Medjool dates
½ C water
⅓ C salted whole peanuts
1 tsp vanilla extract
Set aside another ½ C whole peanuts

Chocolate
1 C vegan chocolate chips
3 Tbsp coconut oil
1 Tbsp smooth all-natural peanut butter

DIRECTIONS

1. For the base, blend all ingredients in food processor until thoroughly smooth. Place parchment paper on 9x9-inch pan. Spread contents evenly. Chill in freezer for 1 hour.

2. For the caramel layer, blend all ingredients in food processor until thoroughly smooth. Spread on top of chilled base. Top another ½ cup of whole salted peanuts on caramel layer. Lightly press into layer. Chill again for 1 more hour, or freeze overnight.

3. For the chocolate layer, microwave vegan chocolate chips and coconut oil for about 1 minute. Remove from microwave, add peanut butter, mix until fully incorporated and smooth. Chill in freezer. Remove your pan from the freezer, and cut 1x3-inch bars. Cover with chocolate by dabbing a spoon of chocolate on parchment paper, and place bar on top of that section (once cooled chocolate will harden and come off nicely). Cover bar with chocolate using a spoon and build on to the sides. Place in freezer to harden for 1 more hour before eating. You can store it in the freezer or fridge depending on whether you want a hard or softer bar. Enjoy!

PEANUT BUTTER & DATE ENERGY BALLS

···« 25~30 Balls »···

I'm a huge fan of dates! Especially Medjool dates; it's like eating creamy caramel. I'm all about creating nutrient- and energy-dense desserts, and these Peanut Butter & Date Energy Balls are a perfect example! And they're so easy to make! The benefits of dates are numerous, but some of the best ones to note are that they are an energy booster, high in antioxidants, and help to reduce inflammation. Combined with the protein found in peanuts and the natural fats in grains such as rolled oats and puffed rice, you have a perfectly balanced macronutrient snack. These can hold in an airtight container in the fridge for weeks to months, since there's no water in the ingredients.

INGREDIENTS

2 C roasted rolled oats
1 ½ C puffed rice
2 C smooth all-natural
   peanut butter
½ C vegan chocolate chips
⅓ C honey or agave
7–8 Medjool dates, pitted
   and mashed
2 Tbsp chia seeds
2 Tbsp coconut oil
1 tsp vanilla extract
½ tsp salt

Coat with
Shredded coconut

DIRECTIONS

1. Spread oats on to a baking tray lined with parchment paper. Place in the oven for 10 minutes at 350 degrees.

2. In a large bowl, place puffed rice, peanut butter, mashed dates, and the remaining ingredients with the vegan chocolate chips on the top. Then pour out the oats while still hot and let it sit over the ingredients for a minute or two. This will cause the vegan chocolate chips to melt slightly. Now, begin to work the ingredients together using a spatula first, then your hands. Squeeze ingredients through your fingers until fully incorporated and partly sticky.

3. Now, begin to press a handful into your hands to form balls that are just under 2 inches wide. Roll onto a plate with shredded coconut and press into the ball. Line in an airtight container.

4. Store in the fridge. These can store very well for several weeks while refrigerated. Enjoy!

··· 183 ···
DESSERTS

ROCKY ROAD
COOKIE DOUGH BARS

MAKES
··· « 16 ~ 20 Bars » ···

USE A 12X12-INCH PAN

One of my favorite memories growing up was on those warm California days, when the chlorine smell from an afternoon's play in the pool with my siblings was still fresh on my skin, and my dad would serve us ice cream on a crispy cone. He would always smile big and raise his eyebrows as he passed on this melting jewel of goodness to our eagerly awaiting hands. We'd eat it sitting on the grass, licking slowly, competing to be the last one to finish. It was always rocky road, his favorite. This recipe is a healthier twist on this classic in honor of those simple yet cherished moments in my life.

INGREDIENTS

Cookie dough
1 ½ C almond flour
½ C coconut flour
¾ C cashew butter, unsalted
⅓ C maple syrup
¾ C roasted almonds,
  roughly chopped
2 C baby vegan marshmallows
2 Tbsp coconut oil
½ tsp vanilla extract
½ tsp salt

Chocolate topping
1 C vegan chocolate chips
3 Tbsp smooth all-natural peanut
  butter
1 Tbsp coconut oil

DIRECTIONS

1. Microwave coconut oil for 20 seconds. In a small bowl, mix the coconut oil with the cashew butter. Then add the maple syrup, vanilla extract, and salt. Set mixture aside.

2. In a larger bowl, mix the almond flour with coconut flour. Then pour coconut oil mixture into larger bowl. Work the ingredients into each other using your hands.

3. Once well incorporated, add the chopped almonds and the baby vegan marshmallows. Continue to work in the ingredients until well incorporated.

4. Line a 12x12-inch baking pan with parchment paper. Press in your cookie dough mixture until you have a flat, tightly packed layer. Place in the freezer to chill for about 15–20 minutes.

5. In the meantime, place your vegan chocolate chips, peanut butter, and coconut oil in a bowl, and place in the microwave for 30 seconds. Mix ingredients. Place the bowl in the microwave for another 30 seconds. At this point, the ingredients should be well melted and mixed thoroughly.

6. Remove your tray from the freezer. Pour the chocolate mixture on top, and spread chocolate evenly. Let sit for a few minutes until perfectly flat. Then chill for 1–2 hours. Cut out desired-size pieces. Serve. Enjoy!

COOKIE DOUGH PEANUT BUTTER BARS

MAKES

···« 20 2x2—inch Bars »···

These bars are bomb! In the words of several of my friends. They're mainly made out of peanut butter and almond flour, making them protein-dense. They also have a secret ingredient. Have you heard of lucuma powder? Lucuma is a high-nutrient Peruvian fruit that has a maple syrup-like flavor, which makes it a great natural sweetener. It's great to throw in smoothies, homemade ice cream, and nut bars.

INGREDIENTS

Cookie dough layer

1 ½ C almond flour
1 C coconut flour
1 C vegan dark chocolate chips, chopped
1 C smooth all-natural peanut butter
6 Tbsp coconut oil
6 Tbsp maple syrup
3 Tbsp lucuma powder
1 tsp vanilla
½ tsp salt

Peanut butter layer

¾ C smooth all-natural peanut butter
½ C peanut butter chips
1 Tbsp coconut oil

DIRECTIONS

1. Mix in all dry ingredients in a large bowl.

2. Melt the coconut oil in a small bowl in the microwave for about 25 seconds. Then add maple syrup and vanilla.

3. Roughly chop the chocolate chips.

4. Add the coconut oil mixture to your large bowl. Incorporate ingredients using your hands. Add the chocolate chips last, and mix until well incorporated.

5. Line a 9x9-inch tray with parchment paper. Press mixture tightly into the tray until well leveled.

6. Microwave peanut butter layer ingredients for about 30 seconds. Mix until smooth. Pour over cookie dough layer, spreading evenly.

7. Place tray in the freezer for 2–3 hours, until firm. Slice into desired bar size. Store in freezer. Enjoy!

   Note: If you can't find a vegan option for peanut butter chips, you can increase the amount of peanut butter to 1 ½ C and add ¼ C maple syrup and 3 Tbsp of coconut oil.

EASY-PEASY REESE'S BARS

MAKES
···« 16 Bars or 32 Minis »···

OK, so Reese's Pieces candy was also one of my childhood favorites, so naturally I just had to learn how to make my own! This is basically peanut butter and coconut flour with dark chocolate chips. It's important to feel good when you're eating food that you love, and that's a part of the wholeness journey we are just now beginning to scratch the surface of. Cheers to the beauty of nutrient-dense treats that are easy to make and wonderful to eat!

INGREDIENTS

Peanut butter layer
1 ¼ C smooth all-natural peanut butter
1 coconut flour
⅓ C maple syrup
½ tsp vanilla extract
¼ tsp salt

Chocolate layer
1 C vegan chocolate chips
½ C smooth all-natural peanut butter
¼ tsp salt

DIRECTIONS

1. For the peanut butter layer, mix in all the ingredients using a spatula. Then begin using your hands, working the ingredients until you have a sticky, consistent mound. Use an 8x8-inch tray for thicker bars, or a 9x9-inch tray for slightly thinner bars. Line your tray with parchment paper, and begin pressing your mixture into the tray until an even, flat layer is formed.

2. For the chocolate layer, microwave your chocolate chips, or melt in a bowl suspended on top of boiling water. Once melted, mix in the peanut butter and salt until fully incorporated and creamy. Pour on top of your peanut butter layer, spreading evenly. Pop in the freezer for about 1 hour.

3. Remove from the freezer, and slice into bars. Store in an airtight container in the fridge. Enjoy!

APRICOT CRUMB BARS

MAKES

···« 14~16 Bars »···

I took a batch of these beautiful treats to one of my last classes of my PhD program and was surprised with how everyone swooned over them. It may have had something to do with the shredded coconut and lemon zest. This recipe has 50% less fat and sugar than that found in most crumb bars, without the compromise on tastiness. Apricot preserves are packed full of flavor and have just the perfect amount of tartness to balance out their sweetness. If you're looking for a lower-calorie pastry that would go beautifully with a cup of herbal tea, then this is your dessert!

INGREDIENTS

Base

Dry
2 C flour
½ C shredded coconut
½ C powdered sugar
¼ tsp baking powder
¼ tsp salt

Wet
1 can coconut milk, solid part
4 Tbsp vegetable shortening
2 tsp lemon zest
1 C apricot preserves

Crumbs
⅓ C of the base dough
¼ C flour

DIRECTIONS

1. Mix wet and dry ingredients separately. Add wet ingredients to dry, and mix well. Once incorporated, remove about ⅓ C of the dough and set aside.

2. Lightly spray oil your baking tray. You can use a 9x9-inch tray for a thicker, moister bar, or a 9x12-inch tray for a thinner bar. Press in the base dough, then scoop on the apricot preserves, spreading evenly on the surface of the dough.

3. For the crumbs, work the flour into the dough you set aside. Use your hands to break apart and crumble your dough. You can also use a knife to run through your crumbs in a chopping manner to make smaller and more even crumbs. Take the crumbs and sprinkle on top of the preserve layer until evenly distributed.

4. Set your oven at 325 degrees, and bake for 30–35 minutes. Crumbs will begin to lightly brown when ready. Set aside to cool before cutting. Cut out desired size of bars. Store in your fridge. Enjoy!

COCONUT PEPPERMINT BONBONS

MAKES
···« Approx. 24 Bonbons »···

These bonbons are so good and healthy it should be illegal to call them candy! Though these are calorie-dense, they are also nutrient-dense since they are mostly made out of nuts. Nuts are a good source of dietary fiber and contain a wide range of essential nutrients, such as B vitamins, vitamin E, and minerals such as calcium, iron, and magnesium. I hope you will enjoy these little holiday-themed creations of mine and that you will be able to share them with the people you love!

INGREDIENTS

Bonbon

1 ½ C shredded coconut
1 ½ C coconut flour
1 C cashew butter
¾ C coconut cream
¾ C maple syrup
3 Tbsp coconut oil
½ tsp peppermint extract
½ tsp vanilla extract
¼ tsp salt

Chocolate

1 C vegan chocolate chips
2 Tbsp smooth all-natural peanut butter
1 Tbsp coconut oil
1 Tbsp dark cocoa powder
A few drops of peppermint extract

Peppermint candy, crushed,
   to lightly top

DIRECTIONS

1. In a bowl, mix in all the ingredients for the bonbons. Use your hands to fully incorporate the ingredients. Line a pan with parchment paper, and use your hands to create 1-inch wide balls. Place balls on the parchment paper, then place in the freezer to chill for 10–15 minutes.

2. Next, in a small bowl, place your chocolate chips, peanut butter, and coconut oil in the microwave for about 40 seconds. Mix until completely melted and smooth. Add the cocoa powder and peppermint extract. Mix until smooth.

3. Remove your tray from the freezer. Now, using a small plate with a piece of parchment paper on it, spoon a little chocolate on to the paper and place one of the balls on it. Then spoon chocolate on to the ball until completely covered. Using two spoons, gently lift the ball and place back on the tray. Repeat until complete. Lightly sprinkle crushed peppermint candy on the top of your bonbons as the chocolate begins to cool.

4. Place tray in the freezer for about 2 hours or so to chill and set. Your bonbons are now ready! Store in the fridge. Since there's no water added, note that they can last for several weeks in the fridge. Enjoy!

CHOCOLATE FUDGE BROWNIES

MAKES

··· « *16 Brownies* » ···

These are truly the perfect nutrient-dense fudge brownies. What makes them so incredibly moist and rich is the ripe avocado hiding amidst decadent chocolate layers. It's true what they say, chocolate makes you happy. I remember the last time I made these I had tripped and scraped both my knees during a jog. It was so bad I could barely bend them for several weeks after that. But I remember treating myself to a handsome helping of these brownies that day and literally smiling from ear to ear from how comforting they were!

INGREDIENTS

Dry

1 ½ C all-purpose flour

½ C crushed walnuts

⅓ C dark cocoa powder

1 tsp baking powder

¼ tsp salt

Wet

1 can coconut milk

1 ripe avocado

6 Medjool dates, placed in hot
   water for 5 minutes

3 ½ Tbsp maple syrup

2 Tbsp coconut oil

1 tsp apple cider vinegar

¼ tsp vanilla extract

Chocolate topping (equal parts)

2 Tbsp dark cocoa powder

2 Tbsp coconut oil

2 Tbsp smooth all-natural peanut
   butter

2 Tbsp maple syrup

DIRECTIONS

1. Mix dry ingredients in a bowl. Place wet ingredients in a food processor, and process until fully incorporated. Add to dry ingredients, and mix using a spatula until incorporated.

2. Line parchment paper in a 9x9-inch pan, and pour out mixture. Set oven to 350 degrees and bake for 25–30 minutes. Place a knife in the center to check if ready. If it comes out clean, turn off heat and remove from oven to cool.

3. For the chocolate topping, place coconut oil in the microwave for about 30 seconds. Mix with remaining ingredients until smooth. Pour onto cooled brownies. Place in the fridge for about half an hour before cutting. Cut into squares. Store in the fridge. Enjoy!

CHOCOLATE-COVERED ALMOND PISTACHIO COOKIES

MAKES
...« 20 Cookies »...

This recipe has been voted as my family's favorite cookie! Then again, who doesn't love a freshly baked cookie that's half dipped in dark chocolate and sprinkled with crushed pistachio? It's mostly made of almond flour and all-natural almond butter. Overall, this cookie might taste and look like your average cookie from the patisserie, but it contains all the nutrients you'd get from a hardy, healthy breakfast!

INGREDIENTS

Dry
½ C all-purpose flour
½ C almond flour
½ tsp baking soda
½ tsp baking powder
¼ tsp salt

Wet
¾ C all-natural almond butter
½ C coconut sugar
2 Tbsp coconut oil
¼ C maple syrup
1 flax-egg (1 Tbsp flaxseed meal +
   3 Tbsp water)
1 tsp vanilla extract
¼ tsp almond extract

Chocolate
2.5 oz vegan dark chocolate bar
1 Tbsp peanut butter
1 Tbsp maple syrup
1 tsp coconut oil

Cookie toppings
Crushed pistachio

DIRECTIONS

1. Start by setting your oven to 350 degrees.

2. For the flax-egg, take the flaxseed meal and mix it with the water, then place in the microwave for 30 seconds. Set aside.

3. Mix the dry ingredients in a bowl. Then mix the wet ingredients in a separate bowl. Now, incorporate both and add in the flax-egg. Mix until fully incorporated.

4. Line a baking tray with parchment paper. Create 1-inch balls by pressing and rolling ingredients in your hands until firm. Place on the trays with enough space to press down two ways using a fork. Place in previously heated oven for 12–13 minutes. Then set aside to cool completely before removing them from the tray.

5. In the meantime, prep your chocolate. Microwave all your ingredients (in increments of 15–20 seconds at a time; may need to repeat 2–3 times) in a small bowl, and mix until fully melted and incorporated.

6. Spoon your melted chocolate on to half of the cookie, letting the extra drip off. Place back on parchment paper. Sprinkle your crushed pistachio on one part of the chocolate-covered section of the cookie. Once done, place the tray in the fridge for about 20 minutes before serving to completely set. Enjoy!

CHOCOLATE CHIP MACADAMIA NUT COOKIES

MAKES
...«*Approx. 20 Cookies*»...

There's nothing quite like a chunky chocolate chip cookie! And I just love including some beautiful macadamia nuts in my cookies. They add such a rich, buttery flare to a variety of desserts and foods. These cookies are super easy to put together and are a great dessert option to look forward to at work or to pack for a picnic. Chocolate and macadamia nuts always manage to make such a beautiful combination!

INGREDIENTS

Dry
1 C flour
½ C almond flour
½ C coconut sugar
¼ C shredded coconut
⅓ C macadamia nuts, roughly chopped
⅓ C vegan chocolate chips
1 tsp baking powder
½ tsp salt

Wet
¼ C coconut oil
¼ C almond milk
3 Tbsp peanut butter
½ tsp vanilla extract
½ tsp apple cider vinegar

DIRECTIONS

1. In a small bowl, melt the coconut oil by placing in the microwave for 20 seconds. Mix until well melted.

2. Add the remaining wet ingredients together in a separate bowl, and mix with the oil until fully incorporated.

3. Mix the dry ingredients, then incorporate with the wet ingredients.

4. Place parchment paper on a baking pan. Make 1.5-inch balls. Press balls into the pan to your desired thickness. If you prefer a moister cookie, leave it at a little less than ½ an inch thick. Set oven to 325 degrees for 15 minutes.

5. Remove from heat, and place on a cooling rack. Then store in an airtight container. Enjoy!

OATMEAL ALMOND COOKIES

MAKES

...« Approx. 20 Cookies »...

If you're a fan of almonds and oats, then you will love these! We're bringing the best of both worlds into one beautiful little place. I love any excuse I can get to use almond extract in my recipes, and this is a perfect example! There's something so irresistible and flowery about almond extract when mixed with just the right amount of sweetness and nuttiness.

INGREDIENTS

Dry
1 C rolled oats
½ C almond flour
½ C flour
½ C shredded coconut
½ C sugar
⅓ C crushed almonds
1 tsp cinnamon
1 tsp baking powder
½ tsp salt

Wet
¾ C almond butter
3 Tbsp coconut oil
2 Tbsp almond milk
2 Tbsp maple syrup
1 tsp apple cider vinegar
½ tsp almond extract
½ tsp vanilla extract

DIRECTIONS

1. Use a spatula to mix wet and dry ingredients together. Then begin to lightly use your hands to work the oil and almond butter into the dough and rolled oats.

2. Create about 1.5-inch balls, and place on parchment paper on a baking tray, leaving about 2 inches between each ball. Press the ball down gently to form cookie shapes.

3. Preheat oven to 325 degrees, and bake cookies for no longer than 15 minutes. Once ready, allow to cool for a few minutes. Store in an airtight container. Enjoy!

Note: The thicker the balls formed, the moister your cookie will be when baking. Forming thinner balls will make them crispier, and they will resemble a granola bar in texture.

KLEICHAT TAMUR

MAKES

··· « *Over 2 Dozen Cookies* » ···

When I was a little girl, I was introduced to Iraq's national cookie. It's called kleichat tamur, which translates to date cookie. I have fond memories of both my grandmother and mother preparing the dough, spreading the date paste, rolling, and cutting out little golden nuggets of date and dough. The smell emanating from the oven as they baked was unforgettable. It was our nonperishable energy snack after long hours of playing in the park with our cousins, and seemed to always be present at large family gatherings. Part of the perks of being born into a culturally diverse family is experiencing all the national foods that come with it!

INGREDIENTS

4 C all-purpose flour
8 oz soft Medjool dates
1 ¼ C warm water
1 ¼ C vegetable oil
1 tsp salt
1 tsp yeast
1 tsp ground cardamom

DIRECTIONS

1. In a small bowl, place the yeast in the warm water, and cover to foam (5–10 minutes).

2. Combine flour, half the ground cardamom, salt, and 1 C oil in a larger bowl, and work together using your hands. Add the yeast and water mixture to the flour mixture. Knead the dough and add more water, if needed. Your dough should be moist, but not sticky. Once done, place in an oiled bowl, cover, and let it rise in a warm place for 1 hour.

3. Cook your dates with ¼ C oil and the remaining cardamom. Cook for about 5–7 minutes on medium heat. Press and mix until well incorporated and softened. Let it cool before using. Cover the cutting board with parchment paper. Spread the dates into a thin layer using a rolling pin, between ⅛–¼ inches.

4. Roll out the dough into similar thickness. Layer the date sheet on top of the dough sheet. Roll the dough like a jelly roll. Make 1-inch cuts, and arrange on parchment paper on a pan. Brush the top with oil, and bake for 30 minutes at 350 degrees.

5. Put the cookies on a cooling rack. Store them in a cookie container or Tupperware. Enjoy!

BAKLAVA

MAKES

···« *Over 2 Dozen Pieces* »···

Nothing defines the sweetness of the Middle East better than authentic baklava. You just need a few simple ingredients to bring this superb dessert to life. If you can manage to get hold of some real orange blossom water, you will be able to raise your baklava to its genuine status. You can find it at most Mediterranean stores, but just in case you don't have one nearby, you can find it on Amazon. This recipe is designed to be lower in sugar and fat than the original, with little compromise on flavor.

INGREDIENTS

Phyllo sheets
16 oz phyllo dough
½ C coconut oil

Stuffing
3 C whole walnuts
½ C sugar
2 Tbsp orange blossom water

Syrup
1 C water
1 C sugar
2 Tbsp orange blossom water
1 Tbsp lemon

DIRECTIONS

1. Thaw your phyllo dough. Then divide it into two sections of 12 sheets, one section for the top, one for the bottom. Start with the bottom. Melt your coconut oil by putting it in the microwave for 40 seconds. Place one sheet on a greased baking pan that fits the phyllo dough dimensions, usually a standard cooking sheet will do. Using a cooking brush, dab coconut oil over the whole sheet, and place a new sheet on top. Repeat until you're done with the 12 sheets. Bake at 350 degrees until golden and slightly risen, about 10–15 minutes or so.

2. Roughly chop walnuts, and mix in your sugar and blossom water. Place on prebaked phyllo layer, layer and start placing the phyllo sheets for the top in the same manner you completed the bottom.

3. Cut into diamond shapes, straight lines from top to bottom, then diagonally. Bake at 350 degrees until golden brown, about 20 minutes or so.

4. For the syrup, mix water, sugar, and lemon in a saucepan, and bring to a boil until thickened into a syrup consistency. At that point, mix in the orange blossom water and allow to cool at room temperature. Then add it directly on to the baked baklava. Allow several minutes for it to soak and seep through the layers.

   Note: *The syrup and the baklava must be at opposite temperatures. If baklava is hot, the syrup should be cooled. If the baklava is cooled, the syrup should be relatively hot. Either way, allow to cool after syrup is poured on to baklava.*

5. Can be stored at room temperature, but I like to keep them in the fridge. They can last several weeks to a few months refrigerated. Enjoy!

BAKED DOUGHNUTS
WITH CHOCOLATE GLAZE

MAKES

···« 6 Doughnuts »···

OK, so you might think I'm stretching it here with vegan baked doughnuts (when usually they contain dairy and are deep-fried), but you might also be pleasantly surprised with how delightfully close these are to old-fashioned doughnuts! You could take this to the next level and substitute the flour with gluten-free flour if you choose. It should taste relatively similar, with only some minor differences with the texture. Even though these are healthier, remember, moderation is key!

INGREDIENTS

Doughnuts

Dry
1 C all-purpose flour
¼ C almond flour
⅓ C sugar
1 Tbsp tapioca powder
1 tsp baking powder
½ tsp baking soda

Wet
¾ C canned coconut milk
2 ½ Tbsp coconut oil
1 Tbsp lemon juice
½ tsp vanilla extract

Chocolate glaze
2 Tbsp coconut oil
2 Tbsp dark cocoa powder
2 Tbsp maple syrup
1 Tbsp all-natural peanut butter

DIRECTIONS

1. Mix dry and wet ingredients separately, then add together and mix until incorporated.

2. Set your oven to 375 degrees. Spray your doughnut baking pan containing 6 cavities. Pour batter in a ziplock bag, then cut one of the tips, and pipe the batter into the molds on your pan. Bake for 10–12 minutes. They should rise quickly since it's a smaller surface area to bake through. Once baked, remove from molds and place on a cooling rack.

3. For the chocolate glaze, place coconut oil and peanut butter together in the microwave for 30–40 seconds. Mix until melted. Add cocoa powder and maple syrup. Mix until smooth.

4. Once the doughnut is cooled, dip the top into a shallow bowl with the chocolate glaze, and then let set. Repeat with remaining doughnuts. Top with crushed roasted almonds, peanuts, or coconut. Let sit in the fridge for about 10 minutes for the glaze to harden. Enjoy!

CARROT CAKE
WITH CASHEW BUTTER GLAZE

MAKES

···« 7—inch Angel Food Pan »···

Perfectly moist carrot cake was always a family favorite growing up. To keep this low-fat version moist without dairy, I used a generous portion of carrots. This loads the cake with vitamins, minerals, and fiber, so "you can have your cake and eat it too." You could also substitute with a little applesauce if you like less carrot in your cake. Taking this cake to the next level with a dimension of "buttery" sweetness is the Cashew Butter Glaze. I hope you enjoy it!

INGREDIENTS

Dry

1 ¾ C all-purpose flour

½ C sugar

4 tsp baking powder

1 ¼ tsp cinnamon

⅓ C walnuts, crushed

1 tsp salt

Wet

1 ½ C shredded carrot

2 flax-eggs (2 Tbsp flaxseed meal
   + 6 Tbsp water)

¾ C almond milk

⅓ C vegetable oil

1 Tbsp maple syrup

2 tsp apple cider vinegar

1 tsp vanilla extract

Cashew butter glaze

3 Tbsp powdered sugar

2 Tbsp cashew butter

2 Tbsp almond milk

1 Tbsp coconut oil

Topping

Crushed walnuts

DIRECTIONS

1. In a small bowl, mix the 6 Tbsp of water with the 2 Tbsp of flaxseed, then put in the microwave for about 35–40 seconds. Mix until it becomes thick and sticky. Set aside.

2. In a bowl, mix the dry ingredients. In another bowl, mix the wet ingredients until well incorporated.

3. Add the wet ingredients to the dry, and mix until partly incorporated. Now, add the flaxseed mixture and lightly mix until incorporated. Do not overmix the batter.

4. Lightly spray oil your pan and dust it with flour. Tap out the excess flour. Now, pour in the batter, and pop in the oven at 350 degrees for 35–40 minutes. Run a knife to the bottom in the center. If it comes out clean it is ready. If not,give it another 5–10 minutes.

5. Once cooled, flip the cake on to a pan or dish upside down for thinner side up and thicker side down.

6. For the glaze, mix ingredients in a small saucepan on medium heat. Mix until boiling. Turn off heat, and let cool slightly. Then pour and spread over bun cake and top with crushed walnuts. Chill for 15–20 minutes before serving. Enjoy!

CHOCOLATE FUDGE CAKE WITH COCONUT ICE CREAM

USE
···«4 Ramekins or 1 9x9—inch Tray»···

When I first made this, the number of "mmmm's" were countless! I was so surprised with how decadent this could be with little to no oil added, no dairy, and half the sugar a fudge cake would usually call for. All the fudginess created here was accomplished with the use of coconut milk and coconut cream. You might have noticed that I sneak in nutrients whenever I can, which explains the almond flour! You might also have noticed that I *do not* count calories in my recipes, and if you're focused on a predominantly plant-based diet and portion control, you shouldn't have to either. Also, because nutrient-dense foods are so satisfying, a little can go a long way!

INGREDIENTS

Cake

Dry
1 C all-purpose flour
½ C almond flour
½ C brown sugar
¼ C dark cocoa powder
2 tsp baking powder
¼ tsp salt
A few dashes cayenne pepper

Wet
1 ¼ C almond milk
½ C coconut cream
1 Tbsp vegetable oil
1 tsp apple cider vinegar
½ tsp vanilla extract

Fudge
1 can coconut milk, solid part only
3–4 Tbsp dark cocoa powder
¼ C maple syrup
2 Tbsp smooth all-natural peanut butter
½ tsp apple cider vinegar
¼ tsp salt
A few dashes of cayenne pepper

Topping
Coconut ice cream

DIRECTIONS

1. For the cake, place dry ingredients in a bowl and mix. Add in wet ingredients, and mix until fully incorporated.

2. Set your oven to 350 degrees. Lightly oil your ramekins (I used 4-inch ramekins) or your baking pan lined with parchment paper. Pour in the batter, and bake for 15–20 minutes, until cooked but slightly still raw in the middle.

3. While baking, prepare your fudge. In a smaller bowl, mix in all your ingredients with a whisk until fully incorporated and smooth.

4. Once the cake is ready, set aside to cool for a few minutes, but still be warm. Lightly dig into the cake with a spoon. Top with generous amounts of fudge, and then ice cream. Enjoy!

CAST-IRON SKILLET BARTLETT PEAR CAKE

FOR A

···《 *10—inch Cake* 》···

I'm pretty obsessed with this cake. Anything baked inside a cast-iron skillet manages to become a showstopper. While developing the recipe, I knew it needed to have an elegant hint of almond extract to pull the flavors together in a unique way, and it did just that! There are two large Bartlett pears hiding in this cake, and it is just marvelous! I recommend topping it with some sort of a coconut cream or coconut ice cream. So good!

INGREDIENTS

Dry

1 C all-purpose flour
½ C almond flour
½ C coconut sugar
1 tsp baking soda
1 tsp baking powder
¼ tsp cinnamon
¼ tsp salt

Wet

1 C almond milk
2 Bartlett pears (ripe, 1 for inside
   the cake, 1 to top)
¼ C vegetable oil
1 ½ Tbsp maple syrup
1 tsp apple cider vinegar
1 tsp lemon zest
½ tsp vanilla extract
¼ tsp almond extract

Topping

1–2 tsp granulated sugar
coconut whip cream
   or nondairy ice cream
candied pecans
powdered sugar

DIRECTIONS

1. Mix dry ingredients in a bowl, and set aside. Take one of your pears, cut out the seeds, slice into chunks, and place in a food processor until small pieces form. Scrape out and mix with wet ingredients.

2. Incorporate wet with dry ingredients. Do not overmix the batter, just mix until well incorporated.

3. Slice your second pear into thin slices, and set aside.

4. Lightly oil your skillet or pan. Pour in the batter, and top with slices of pear in desired pattern. Sprinkle a little granulated sugar and cinnamon. Bake in the oven at 350 degrees for about 35–40 minutes or until baked through. Check the cake by placing a knife in the center. If it comes out clean, it's ready. If not, give it another 5–10 minutes.

5. Once ready, set aside to cool. Sprinkle powdered sugar and top with coconut cream, or your favorite nondairy ice cream. Enjoy!

PUMPKIN SPICE "CHEESECAKE"

SERVES
··· « 10 ~ 12 » ···

The secret to creating delicious yet healthy food is switching out the ratio of what normally constitutes popular, unhealthy foods. For example, a regular cheesecake might contain around 80 percent fat and sugar and just 20 percent (or less) of actual wholesome food. If you switch out this ratio and make 80 percent of your cheesecake out of wholesome foods (such as raw nuts), you have some wiggle room with the 20 percent to turn into something pretty tasty. That's what this cheesecake represents, nutrient-dense, delicious, sweet, and amazingly silky.

INGREDIENTS

Pumpkin spice layer
1 ½ C almond flour
1 C coconut flour
1 can pumpkin puree
¾ C cashew butter
¼ C maple syrup
3 Tbsp coconut oil
3 Tbsp coconut sugar
1 tsp cinnamon
1 tsp vanilla extract
¼ tsp ground ginger
¼ tsp nutmeg
¼ tsp salt

Cream "cheese" layer
1 C raw cashews, soaked for 1–2 hours
1 can coconut milk, solid part only
¼ C maple syrup
1 Tbsp lemon juice
½ tsp vanilla extract
⅛ tsp salt

Topping
Candied pecans

DIRECTIONS

1. First, place your coconut milk can in the freezer for 20 minutes or so to separate the layers (you will use the cream part only, and discard the fluid).

2. In a bowl, mix in all ingredients for your pumpkin layer. Use your hands to fully incorporate. Once ready, line a 9x9-inch baking pan with parchment paper (if you use a slightly larger pan, it should be fine, just note the bars will be a little thinner). Press your mixture into the pan for a flat, smooth surface. Place in the freezer to chill for 20 minutes.

3. Place all ingredients for the cream "cheese" layer into a Vitamix or high-speed blender. Blend until perfectly smooth and creamy. Remove your tray from the freezer, and pour cream on top, spreading evenly. Place back in the freezer to chill and set for at least 2–3 hours before serving.

4. Top with candied pecans. Slice out desired shape size. Store in the fridge for frequent use, or freezer for longer periods of time, just allow to thaw for a few minutes before serving. Enjoy!

ULTIMATE APPLE PIE

SERVES

··· « 6 ⁓ 8 » ···

8-INCH PIE PAN

I'm not trying to brag, but this is literally one of the best apple pies I've ever had, which is why I affectionately named it Ultimate Apple Pie. All the flavor you want in an apple pie is there, with the added fun of less than 3 Tbsp of sugar in the whole thing! And that's because we're harnessing the natural sweetness present in Fuji apples to give us the sweetness we need. You could also use honeycrisp or pink lady apples as well. Top a warm slice with some ice cream and a touch of fresh thyme, and you can kiss your dessert free days goodbye!

INGREDIENTS

Crust
1 ½ C flour
½ C almond flour
4 Tbsp vegetable shortening
3 Tbsp vegetable oil
3 Tbsp water
1 tsp sugar
½ tsp salt

Filling
4–5 Fuji apples, cut into
  ½-inch slices
2 ½ Tbsp sugar
2 Tbsp lemon
2 Tbsp cornstarch
1 Tbsp water
1 tsp apple cider vinegar
½ tsp cinnamon
¼ tsp salt
¼ tsp lemon zest
A few dashes of ground ginger

Topping
Vanilla bean or coconut ice cream

DIRECTIONS

1. For the crust, begin by mixing in dry ingredients, then mix in the shortening and oil. Use your hands to fold in the mixture. Add water one tsp at a time, and continue to fold and press your dough until no loose flour is in the bowl. Wrap with plastic wrap, and place in the fridge for 25–30 minutes.

2. In the meantime, peel and cut your apples. Throw them into a small pot, and add remaining ingredients. Cook for about 5–7 minutes over medium-high heat. Apples should be half cooked. Turn off heat, and cover with lid.

3. Remove your dough from the fridge, and divide into two parts. Place on a lightly flour-dusted counter. Press, and begin rolling into thin layers. For the first part, cut out about a 9-inch circle. Press it into your pan, and pinch to form the pie edges. For the second part, I chose to create small leaves. I did so by cutting out each one with a knife, but there are leaf cookie cutters you can purchase. Or follow any other pattern you like.

4. Pour in the pie filling. Place leaves in circular motion on the surface of the filling in your preferred style. Bake at 375 degrees for 15–20 minutes, until golden brown, or until dough is cooked through. Set aside to cool. Top with you ice cream of choice. Enjoy!

Note: I like the apples in my pie to still have some resistance and be a little firm. If you prefer softer apples, then decrease your baking temperature to 350 degrees, and bake for 25–30 minutes.

BERRY DELICIOUS PIE

SERVES

···« 6 ~ 8 »···

10-INCH PIE PAN

This is a light classic treat that is super easy to make, and even more fun to present and share. Most of this pie is straight-up fruit, so it's hard not to please your body and your taste buds. Berries are wonderful because they are a great source of fiber and contain anti-inflammatory and anticancer properties. Loaded with antioxidants and vitamins, these little bubbles of sweet and tart juices are the perfect ingredient to build your healthier dessert options around.

INGREDIENTS

Crust
1 pack graham crackers
¾ C flour
½ C crushed pecans
¼ C water
3 Tbsp vegetable shortening
2 Tbsp coconut oil
¼ tsp salt

Fruit
20 oz mixed berries, frozen
2 ½ Tbsp tapioca powder
½ C grape juice or apple juice
¼ C sugar
¼ C water
1 ½ tsp apple cider vinegar
2 tsp lemon juice
¼ tsp orange blossom water

Topping
Cashew ice cream

DIRECTIONS

1. Throw graham crackers and pecans in a food processor until fine. In a bowl, mix with flour, then add water, vegetable shortening, coconut oil, and salt. Use your hands to work in the ingredients until well incorporated. Add a little more water if it's too dry and crumbly. Form and press into your pie pan. Preheat your oven to 325 degrees, and bake your crust halfway for about 10 minutes. When done, set aside.

2. Place the mixed berries in a small pot on medium heat. Pour juice, water and tapioca powder into a Mason jar. Close with lid, and shake until mixed, with no lumps. Add to the pot. Add the remaining ingredients, and mix. Cook for about 10–15 minutes, until the sauce thickens, mixing occasionally.

3. When ready, pour your berry mix into your pie crust. Then bake for about 30–35 minutes at 350 degrees. Once done, set aside to cool. Then chill in the fridge for 1 hour or so. Slice and serve with your favorite vanilla ice cream, or in this case, cashew ice cream. Enjoy!

GRAPEFRUIT COCONUT CREAM TART

MAKES

···« 4 Mini Tarts or 1 Standard Tart »···

Where do I begin with how wonderful this dessert is? I'm not a big fan of grapefruit, but I know a lot of people who are, and for good reason, since it is a powerhouse of antioxidants. So I wanted to devote at least one dessert to this beautiful yet often misunderstood fruit. This turned out so elegant, and is a lot easier to put together than it looks! The crust is gluten free and made predominantly of nuts and dates. The cream layer is made mainly out of coconut milk, and the top gel layer is made out of freshly squeezed grapefruit juice.

INGREDIENTS

Crust
1 ½ C almond flour
½ C pecans, ground
5 Medjool dates, pitted
3 Tbsp coconut oil
¼ tsp salt

Cream filling
1 can coconut cream
3 Tbsp cornstarch
⅓ C granulated sugar
1 Tbsp lemon juice
½ tsp vanilla extract

Grapefruit gel
1 C freshly squeezed grapefruit juice
2 Tbsp maple syrup
1 ½ Tbsp cornstarch

Topping
Crushed pistachios

DIRECTIONS

1. For the crust, start by placing the Medjool dates in warm water for about 5 minutes to soften them. Squeeze out the excess water using your hands. Place the ground pecans and the Medjool dates in a food processor, and process until granulated and well incorporated. In a bowl, mix this with the almond flour, coconut oil, and salt. You may need to melt your coconut oil first if it's too hard. You can use your hands to better incorporate the ingredients.

2. I used tart molds that are sized 4.5-inches in diameter. You could also use the larger standard-sized tart mold with the same recipe. Divide into 4 equal parts, and begin forming your crust in the tart mold. Press evenly until uniform surface is achieved. Place tart crusts in the oven at 325 degrees, and bake for about 10 minutes. Then set aside to cool.

3. For the cream filling, place about ¼ C of the coconut cream in a small bowl with the cornstarch, and mix thoroughly until well incorporated. In a small pot, mix in all the ingredients, except for the lemon, and continue to mix on medium heat until it begins to boil (about 3–5 minutes). Once boiling, set to a simmer, and mix until thickened. Once thick, remove from heat, mix in the lemon, and now scoop directly onto the crust, spreading evenly. Place in the fridge to chill and set.

4. For the grapefruit gel, you'll need 2 grapefruits to get 1 C of juice. Pour your juice through a strainer to remove the pulp. Mix ¼ C of the juice with your cornstarch. Ensure you have no starchy lumps. Once ready, place in a small pot with the remaining juice and the maple syrup, and set to medium heat while mixing. Once boiling, set to a simmer, and mix until you notice it's beginning to thicken (about 1–2 minutes). Remove from heat. Now, pull out your tarts from the fridge, and pour out your grapefruit layer. Let chill again for about 1–2 hours before serving. Top with crushed pistachios. Enjoy!

MINI FRUIT TARTS

MAKES

···« *24 Mini Tarts* »···

USE A MINI CUPCAKE TRAY

How adorable are these? Fruit tarts are one of my favorite desserts, so you can imagine how much more I like it when they're practically bite-size! I wanted to make something that had a rich and nutty crust that would balance with a smooth, creamy filling topped with sweet berries, and this hit the spot! Never mind that the cream base is made out of tofu, I like to throw in my protein where I can! This dessert is perfect for a finger-food-themed brunch or a tea party.

INGREDIENTS

Crust
1 pack graham crackers
½ C pecans
3 Tbsp coconut oil
4 Tbsp water
3 Tbsp flour
¼ tsp salt

Cream
1 pack soft tofu
¼ C maple syrup
2 Tbsp sugar
1 tsp apple cider vinegar
1 tsp orange blossom
    water (optional)
Juice of ½ a lemon
½ tsp lemon zest
Pinch of salt

Glaze
¼ C water
2 Tbsp powder sugar
2 tsp lemon juice
1 tsp starch

Fruit
Berries or fruit of your choice

DIRECTIONS

1. Place graham crackers and pecans in a food processor until grainy. Place in a bowl, then add water and coconut oil. Use your hands to work in the ingredients until you have no loose pieces.

2. Lightly spray oil your cupcake tray. Mold your tart crust into the cups. Once done, place in the oven at 350 degrees for about 15 minutes, until lightly browned around the edges. Set aside to cool.

3. For the cream, run soft tofu in a food processor until smooth, then add all the remaining ingredients, and process until fully incorporated and creamy.

4. For the glaze, place contents in a small saucepot on medium heat. Use a whisk to mix until thickened.

5. Pipe your cream into the tarts, and top with berries and fruit of your choice. Then lightly dab with your glaze. Enjoy!

BLUEBERRY SCONES WITH LEMON ZEST

MAKES
···« *8 slices* »···

One of my husband's favorite things to have, which he rarely ever indulges in, is scones. When he first shared how much he liked this pastry, I was determined to make a healthier version of it and baffle him with the results. And this surely did just that! It's still a scone, but with a lot less sugar and fat. I'm not so much a fan of scones, but I must say I was quite happy with these. The combination of blueberry and lemon zest married each other just beautifully in this recipe!

INGREDIENTS

Dry
2 C flour
1 Tbsp brown sugar
1 ½ tsp baking powder
½ tsp salt

Wet
1 can coconut milk, firm part only
⅓ C blueberries
3 Tbsp water
2 Tbsp coconut oil
1 Tbsp vegetable oil
1 ½ tsp lemon zest
1 tsp apple cider vinegar
½ tsp vanilla extract

Serve with
Maple syrup or jam

DIRECTIONS

1. Start by mixing dry ingredients and wet ingredients separately (except for water and blueberries; leave for the last step). Melt coconut oil in the microwave for about 30 seconds.

   Note: *If your canned coconut milk isn't the kind that separates, even when put in the fridge overnight, just make sure it's mixed, and administer half of the can to your mixture, which is about 1 C. In this case, you do not need to add 3 Tbsp of water.*

2. Incorporate wet ingredients with dry. Fold gently, and try not to overwork the dough.

3. Now, add water one tsp at a time. Continue to fold gently. Your dough should be moist, but not sticky. At this point, add the blueberries by gently folding them into the dough. If it is too sticky, add a tsp or so of flour.

4. On a pan with parchment paper, shape your dough into a rough circle about 9 inches across and 1 inch or so high. Now, add a few extra blueberries by pressing them into the top of the dough.

5. Lightly brush some cooking oil on the surface, then sprinkle about 2 tsp granulated sugar, this will harden into a beautiful thin, crispy layer.

6. Use a sharp knife to gently cut the dough into "pizza" slices, leave dough intact.

7. Preheat your oven to 350 degrees, and bake for 25–30 minutes if prefer it little moist. Bake for an extra 10 minutes if you prefer a dryer scone, with crispier edges. Set aside to cool for a few minutes. Slice again, and serve with maple syrup or jam. Enjoy!

CHOCOLATE AVOCADO PUDDING

SERVES
···« 4 ⁓ 6 »···

I know I've said it before about other dessert recipes, but this is by far the most decadent and enticing star of them all! I literally couldn't stop smiling when I first scooped up a cool, rich spoonful of this remarkable pudding into my mouth. Avocados are such a gift from heaven! So rich and so easily manipulated to blend perfectly with either savory or sweet flavors. Avocados are known to have anti-inflammatory properties, and dark cocoa powder is loaded with antioxidants, so together these two make quite a power couple!

INGREDIENTS

2 ripe avocados
2 cans coconut milk, solid
    part only
½ C maple syrup
4–5 Medjool dates, soaked
    and drained
¼ C dark cocoa powder
3 Tbsp smooth all-natural peanut
    butter
½ tsp vanilla extract
½ tsp apple cider vinegar
¼ tsp salt
A dash of cayenne pepper

Topping
Fresh berries
Crushed roasted almonds

DIRECTIONS

1. For your canned coconut milk, either place the can in the fridge overnight, or in the freezer for about 30 minutes so that the layers can be well separated.

2. Place all ingredients in a food processor, and process until smooth and creamy.

3. Chill for 1–2 hours before serving.

4. Top with fresh berries and crushed almonds, and serve. Enjoy!

MANGO COCONUT CREAM PUDDING

SERVES
··· « 4 ⁓ 6 » ···

Sweet, tart mango and creamy coconut flavors go so perfectly together! This smooth, silky dessert is so tasty and so easy to make, you can get it done in just 10 minutes. Coconuts have truly empowered the plant-based community to reproduce the creamy textures that can usually only be created using animal products or highly processed nonanimal products.

INGREDIENTS

2 ripe mangoes, peeled and cut
1 C frozen mango chunks
2 cans coconut milk, solid part only
1 ½ Tbsp tapioca + 3 Tbsp hot water
Juice of one lime
¼ C maple syrup
   (add more as desired)
½ tsp vanilla extract
½ tsp lime zest
¼ tsp Himalayan sea salt

Cream Topping
1 can coconut milk, solid part only
2 Tbsp maple syrup
½ tsp vanilla extract

Topping
Crushed pistachios

DIRECTIONS

1. Chill your coconut milk cans in the freezer for 30 minutes in order to separate the layers, or leave them in the fridge overnight.

2. Use a food processor to blend the frozen and ripe mango and the coconut milk solid.

3. When smooth, add in maple syrup, lime juice, lime zest, vanilla, and sea salt. Process well.

4. Mix the tapioca with hot water until thickened. Add to the mixture, and process until incorporated

5. Chill in the fridge for 1–2 hours.

6. For the cream topping, mix the ingredients in a bowl. Chill in fridge for 1–2 hours.

7. Style as desired, and top with crushed pistachios. Enjoy!

TART STRAWBERRY SORBET

MAKES

···« 6 Scoops »···

Sorbet is such a fancy way to have your frozen fruit. I will say this does take a little work to put together, but it is well worth the effort! My husband and I are obsessed with this recipe, and more so with the lack of guilt it comes with. If you follow the instructions, this sorbet becomes almost creamy in consistency because you would have broken down the ice crystals to very small pieces. If you have an ice cream machine, more power to you! But this was created the old-fashioned way, with heaps of love, hand scraping, and churning.

INGREDIENTS

3 C frozen strawberries
⅓ C almond milk
3 Tbsp maple syrup
2 Tbsp lemon juice
1 ½ tsp apple cider vinegar
½ tsp lemon zest
¼ tsp salt

DIRECTIONS

1. Throw all ingredients into a Vitamix or high-speed blender. Use a tamper to work into the blade. Once well incorporated, blend until flow is created and consistency is smooth.

2. Pour into a shallow Tupperware or Pyrex container. Make sure to use a container size that allows you to spread out the mix to be 1-inch or so high. This will help it freeze more consistently.

3. Place in the freezer. After 2 hours, churn the contents. (I did this using a spoon and scraping and reforming into a packed 1-inch layer.) Repeat this process two more times.

4. Let it freeze overnight. Then churn one more time, and press back into the container. Freeze again for 1 hour. Once done, it should be ready to serve and scoop out, just like ice cream. Enjoy!

Note: You can replicate this recipe with blueberries, raspberries, mangoes, or combinations of those.

Smoothies

& Drinks

SALTED CHOCOLATE PEANUT BUTTER SMOOTHIE

SERVES

··· « 2 ⌣ 3 » ···

Put peanut butter, chocolate, and banana together anytime, anywhere, and I'll be one happy camper. This smoothie can be breakfast or dessert as far as I'm concerned. All-natural peanut butter is an excellent plant-based source of protein, vitamins, and minerals. For me, it's always been so fun to use presentation as a way to trick my mind into thinking I'm indulging in a scandalous dessert. I encourage you to experiment and have fun with this since, believe it or not, how we see and enjoy our food plays a role in our overall wholeness!

INGREDIENTS

Smoothie
2 large ripe bananas,
   preferably frozen
2 C almond milk
2–3 Tbsp all-natural peanut butter
¼ tsp vanilla extract
¼ tsp of sea salt

Chocolate syrup
2 Tbsp coconut oil
2 Tbsp maple syrup
1 Tbsp dark cocoa powder
1 Tbsp all-natural peanut butter

Topping
Crushed peanuts
Sea salt

DIRECTIONS

1. For the smoothie, throw ingredients into a Vitamix or high-speed blender.

2. For the syrup, place coconut oil in the microwave for about 30 seconds. Mix until melted. Add the cocoa powder, maple syrup, and peanut butter. Mix thoroughly. Place in a squeeze bottle with a narrow tip (used for decorating the inside of your smoothie jar before pouring in the smoothie).

3. Pour the smoothie into your jar. Drizzle more chocolate syrup on top as desired. Top with crushed peanuts and sea salt. Enjoy!

CREAMY RASPBERRY SMOOTHIE

VEGAN

SERVES

···《 2～3 》···

Raspberries are a delightful treat to work with. I love the tart, heavenly flavors they give off. Raspberries are high in antioxidants and vitamin C. These play an important role in their anti-inflammatory properties. This smoothie can be prepared as a breakfast option or an afternoon snack. I personally prefer frozen over fresh berries for smoothies. They're easier to stock up on, and last a lot longer! Also, research has shown frozen berries to deliver a higher dose of antioxidants than fresh, and, best of all, they're cheaper!

INGREDIENTS

2 C almond milk
2 frozen ripe bananas
1 C frozen raspberries
3 Medjool dates
2 Tbsp cashew butter
½ C water or ice (optional)

Topping
Crushed almonds, or nut of choice

DIRECTIONS

1. To make a gradient, just divide your raspberries by the number of serving containers you're going to use (recommend 3–4 parts).

2. Start with the lightest color, with ¼ of the raspberries thrown into your high-speed blender or Vitamix with the remaining ingredients. Pour into your first glass, then add another ¼ of the raspberries to the mix. Blend, and pour into a second glass, and so on.

3. If you don't care for the gradients, then just toss in all the ingredients into your blender, and you're done! Add water or ice if it's too thick for your liking.

4. Top with crushed almonds or nut of choice, and serve. Enjoy!

BERRY-LICIOUS OAT SMOOTHIE

MAKES
···« *2 Short Mason Jars* »···

This is my husband's go-to breakfast request on mornings when he's on the run. It tastes delicious, hydrates, and keeps him energized until his lunch break. It effortlessly includes all the macronutrients (healthy fats, protein, and carbohydrates) and best part for me is . . . it takes two minutes to put together!

INGREDIENTS

2 frozen ripe bananas
2 C almond milk
5–6 frozen strawberries
½ C frozen blueberries
3 Tbsp rolled oats
1 handful walnuts
3 Medjool dates
½ C ice

Topping
Chia seeds (optional)
Fruit (optional)

DIRECTIONS

1. Start by first throwing the oats and walnuts into a high-speed blender or Vitamix, and blend until powdered.

2. Add the rest of the ingredients, and blend until fully incorporated.

3. Optional, top with fruit and chia seeds. Enjoy!

THE HULK SMOOTHIE

MAKES
···« *2 Short Mason Jars* »···

Green smoothies are the best! The idea is to load the smoothie with vitamin-packed greens (like spinach or kale), and then mask it with the natural sweetness and flavors of fruits, such as banana and mango. This smoothie is rich with antioxidants and iron. You can increase your protein by adding all-natural peanut butter or almond butter. It adds a level of richness, and I personally prefer that over protein powders. This smoothie works great as a hydrating pick-me-up, breakfast option, or post-workout energy booster.

INGREDIENTS

1 large ripe banana
1 C frozen spinach
1 C frozen mango
1 C almond milk
½ C coconut water
2 Tbsp almond butter
3 Medjool dates
½ C crushed ice

DIRECTIONS

1. Throw contents into a high-speed blender or Vitamix.

2. Blend until smooth.

3. Add or decrease coconut water for desired consistency. Serve immediately. Enjoy!

CARROT GINGER SMOOTHIE

MAKES
···« 2 Short Mason Jars »···

I've always been a fan of carrot juice, so you can think about this drink like carrot juice on steroids. This smoothie is super refreshing and loaded with vitamin A and antioxidants. Ginger is an amazing anti-inflammatory agent, and is known to have medicinal properties. I love it because it adds a nice kick! Ginger can even help to reduce muscle pain and soreness. So if you need a boost, and yesterday was leg day, then this might be exactly what you're looking for!

INGREDIENTS

1 ½ C almond milk

1 large ripe banana

1 C chopped carrots

3 Medjool dates

2 Tbsp cashew butter

½ C crushed ice

1 tsp ginger powder, or minced
   fresh ginger

DIRECTIONS

1. Throw contents into a high-speed blender or Vitamix.

2. Blend until smooth.

3. Add or decrease ice for desired consistency. Serve immediately. Enjoy!

SPIRULINA ALMOND SMOOTHIE

MAKES

···« 3 ~ 4 Cups »···

Spirulina, which is a blue-green microalgae, is quite an impressive superfood! One teaspoon contains a whopping 2,800% more beta-carotene (the precursor for vitamin A) than that found in carrots. It's also an excellent source of K1, K2, B12, iron, and contains loads of phytonutrients. Not to mention that one serving is 60% protein. There's a lot of fun ways to incorporate spirulina in your smoothies, but I wanted to highlight its beautiful ocean-blue hue, so here's how to shake it up!

INGREDIENTS

2 frozen ripe bananas
2 C almond milk
½ C crushed ice
3–4 Medjool dates
2 Tbsp almond butter
¼–½ tsp spirulina
½ tsp lemon zest

Toppings
Shredded coconut
Lemon zest

DIRECTIONS

1. Throw ingredients into a high-speed blender or Vitamix. Blend until smooth.

2. To increase color gradient, add ¼ tsp more spirulina to your smoothie for darker, bolder color.

3. Top with shredded coconut and lemon zest, and serve. Enjoy!

HOT CHOCOLATE

SERVES
···« 2 ⁓ 3 »···

There's nothing quite like sipping on a cup of hot chocolate, snuggled on a couch, staring out the window on a cold winter's day. I love how simple, seemingly insignificant moments like that can warm our hearts and remind us of the importance of slowing down and letting ourselves get lost in our minds. So, here's a healthier twist in honor of the muse-worthy classic hot chocolate drink we all know and love.

INGREDIENTS

2 ½ C almond milk
2 Tbsp cocoa powder
3 Tbsp vegan chocolate chips
2 Tbsp agave syrup or
   maple syrup
1 Tbsp smooth all-natural peanut
   butter
¼ tsp vanilla extract
Pinch of salt

Toppings
Vegan marshmallows
Cocoa powder
Chocolate drizzle

DIRECTIONS

1. Whisk your cocoa powder in about ½ C of the almond milk to get rid of any clumps.

2. Place all the ingredients in a teapot. Mix until ingredients have dissolved, and chocolate chips have melted. Pour into glass or mug. Top with vegan marshmallows and cocoa powder. If you need it to be sweeter, add more syrup to your liking. If you want it less sweet, dilute with almond milk.

3. For the drizzle, just melt 2–3 Tbsp of the chocolate chips in the microwave for about 1 minute. Mix until melted. You can also add a little coconut oil to thin it out. Enjoy!

GOLDEN MILK

MAKES
··· « *2 Cups* » ···

You've probably heard of the countless benefits of turmeric. Curcumin is the most active compound of turmeric, and is known to be a potent anti-inflammatory and antioxidant compound. Studies show its medicinal qualities can help to manage depression and even improve symptoms of arthritis. Turmeric has an earthy, musty flavor and tastes almost like what walking on freshly cultivated soil smells like. It's an acquired taste, but you can definitely grow to love it. Golden milk has become all the rage, and this my twist on it.

INGREDIENTS

2 C almond milk
1 ½ Tbsp maple syrup
1 tsp turmeric
¼ tsp vanilla extract
¼ tsp ground ginger
A few dashes of cinnamon
A few dashes of cardamom

DIRECTIONS

1. Heat your milk. Then add the ingredients, and mix. Once well incorporated, turn off the heat, and let it sit for a minute or two. Mix again. The turmeric and other spices will have a tendency to settle to the bottom.

2. Top with a few dashes of cinnamon.

3. You can also have it iced. I love it either way. Enjoy!

PEANUT BUTTER MOCHA

NO CAFFEINE

MAKES

···« *2 ~ 3 Cups* »···

Though I don't drink coffee, one of my favorite smells in a café or coffee shop is just that, the ground coffee! It has a perfumed earthiness to it and instantly makes me feel cozy. For those preferring to steer away from caffeine, there's a wide variety of herbal coffee and mocha mixes now available that you can get from most health-food stores or online. I used a mocha version that is made out of herbs, nuts, and fruit. You can treat it the same way you would normal coffee, or just boil it and then strain it, either way works. By now you'll know I love peanut butter, so you'll find some in here as well.

INGREDIENTS

2 C water
1 heaped Tbsp mocha
1 ½ Tbsp maple syrup
1 Tbsp all natural peanut butter
¼ tsp vanilla
A few dashes of sea salt

Add milk, cream source, or
   cream of your choice

DIRECTIONS

1. What I like to do is put my mocha mix directly into the water, then pass it through a strainer before serving.

2. Boil your mocha with the water for about 3 minutes. Then add the remaining ingredients, and mix until well incorporated. Let it sit for a few minutes to absorb all the layers of flavor. Strain into your cups, leaving about ¼ of the cup empty for your milk or cream choice.

3. You can use either a plant-based milk or even coconut cream. Either will taste great. Add or decrease sweetness to your liking. Enjoy!

RASPBERRY JALAPEÑO SPRITZER

NONALCOHOLIC

MAKES

····« *4 Cups* »····

I can't say enough how much I love this spunky drink! Raspberries are my favorite of the berry family. I love the sharp flavors of sweet and tart balanced perfectly in the cutest little package, with anti-inflammatory properties and vitamin-boosting benefits included. I personally don't drink alcohol, so I wanted to create a series of "mocktails" that are just as beautiful as they are tasty, with a natural kick! Here we used the feisty jalapeño to achieve that. You can strain your juice after you blend it, but I prefer to hold on to the pulp. That's where all the good stuff is!

INGREDIENTS

Concentrated juice
1 C frozen raspberries
1 jalapeño, deseeded
3 Tbsp granulated sugar
Juice of one lime
5–6 mint leaves
¾ C carbonated water

Add
2 C carbonated water
Crushed ice
Infused fresh raspberries
Mint
Jalapeño

DIRECTIONS

1. If you prefer a less spicy drink, use half the jalapeño, just make sure to deseed it. Place the ingredients for the concentrated juice in a high-speed blender or Vitamix, and blend until smooth.

2. Add about ⅓ C of the concentrated juice to ½ C of the carbonated water in a cup with crushed ice. Adjust the carbonated water amount per your desired sweetness level.

3. Style with mint and jalapeño with infused raspberries. Cheers!

PIÑA COLADA

NONALCOHOLIC

MAKES

··· « 4 Cups » ···

The classic piña colada! Recreated, alcohol-free, but not free of the glorious tropical flavors. I used fresh, ripe pineapple instead of processed juice, and I would highly recommend sticking with coconut cream over coconut milk. It gives the drink an elegant richness. The kick here is from the fresh ginger. It complements the flavors beautifully and, surprisingly, is not overpowering. I love how the lime juice adds the perfect amount of acid to the sweet and creamy flavors playing around. Among the "mocktails," this is my husband's favorite. Then again, what's not to love?

INGREDIENTS

1 C ripe pineapple chunks
1 C coconut cream
1 C coconut water
2–3 Tbsp granulated sugar
1 ½ Tbsp lime juice
1 tsp fresh ginger, minced
½ tsp vanilla extract

Add
Crushed ice
Shredded coconut
Pineapple slices

DIRECTIONS

1. Place the ingredients in a high-speed blender or Vitamix, and blend until smooth.

2. Add desired amount of crushed ice to your cup. Pour piña colada, and top with shredded coconut and pineapple slices. Cheers!

GRAPEFRUIT GINGER SPRITZER

NONALCOHOLIC

MAKES
⋯《 4 ⁓ 6 Cups 》⋯

Although I'm not hugely a fan of grapefruit, I love how unexpectedly pleasant this turned out. Vanilla has a way of elevating acidic and bitter flavors, almost like putting a blanket of creaminess on whatever it's added to. Combined with hints of ginger, this makes quite an elegant drink. I love infusing fresh herbs here, like rosemary, or you could use fresh thyme, and, even better, lavender! They manage to pair beautifully with the all the strong flavors going on. You can't help but feel ultraposh sipping on this lovely drink in a chic cocktail glass.

INGREDIENTS

Juice of 3 red grapefruits
3 Tbsp agave syrup
1 2 tsp fresh ginger, minced
Juice of ½ a lemon
1 tsp vanilla extract
2 C carbonated water

Add
Crushed ice
fresh rosemary and blackberries

DIRECTIONS

1. Place ingredients in a high-speed blender or Vitamix, and blend.

2. Adjust the carbonated water amount according to your desired sweetness level.

3. Infuse fresh rosemary and blackberries. Cheers!

STRAWBERRY DAIQUIRI

NONALCOHOLIC

MAKES
···« 4 Cups »···

When I was a little girl, seven or eight years old, one of my mother's cousins was getting married, and I remember it being the fanciest wedding I'd ever been to at the time. It took place on a luxurious resort on the beach. They had little booths of open bars available for the guests. My siblings and I were told we could go to one of the nice men with the bow ties and ask them for a drink. It was the first time I learned what a virgin strawberry daiquiri was. I was smitten, to say the least. I carefully held on to that beautifully decorated glass cup, feeling ultra grown-up, and tickled that these sharp young men trusted us kids with that one drink. Little did they know their kindness would be taken advantage of for the rest of the evening. Here's my twist on that little rascal of a memory.

INGREDIENTS

1 ½ C strawberries, fresh or frozen
1 C coconut water
1 C carbonated water
Juice of 1 large lime
3 Tbsp agave syrup
A few dashes of cayenne pepper

Add
Crushed ice
Infuse with fresh thyme

DIRECTIONS

1. Place the ingredients in a high-speed blender or Vitamix, and blend.

2. Add or decrease carbonated water to adjust sweetness.

3. Pour on to crushed ice, and garnish and infuse with fresh thyme. Cheers!

INDEX

SMOOTHIES & DRINKS

ACKNOWLEDGEMENTS

Special thanks to my incredible mother who, from the first photos and culinary pieces I presented her with, always encouraged me, regardless of how pitiful they were! To my wonderful father for his witty comments, positive reassurance, and being a critical taste tester. To my gracious husband for always supporting my visions and dreams about food, health, and photography. I love you so much. To my sister and brother, thank you for being so encouraging about this project and the many others I've done before. Everyone needs the type of honesty and realness in their life that you both have always given me. To Mike, my early mentor, thank you for believing in my work from the very beginning and for all the counsel and guidance on defining my style and managing my clients.

Notes:

Notes:

Notes:

Notes:

Notes:

Notes:

Notes:

Notes:

Notes: